A HIDDEN Heart

Arketa Williams

Copyright © 2018 by Arketa Williams.

All rights reserved.

No part of this book may be reproduced or transmitted in any form or by any means, electronic or mechanical, including photocopying, recording, or by any information storage and retrieval system, without permission in writing from the copyright author, except for the use of brief quotations in a book review.

Published in the United States by Pen2Pad Ink Publishing.

Requests to publish work from this book or to contact the author should be sent to: contact@pen2padink.org

Arketa Williams retains the rights to all images

Interior design: Pen2Pad Ink Publishing

Rev. date: 5/18/2018

Acknowledgements

From the bottom of my heart I would like to say thank you to all of you that supported, encouraged, motivated, and inspired me throughout this process. Thank you to those of you that forced me to break through my solitude of silence and write, dream, and speak again.

To Vanessa Ingram, De'borah Carter, Rev. Linda Curry, and Soneakqua White each of you unknowingly tagged team in such a way that I had no choice but to move forward, learn, grow, and get better. Thank you. Each time I had a question or a problem I couldn't solve you were right there. Thank you for your prayers and conversations. For that I am forever grateful. Thank you for believing in me when I didn't even believe in myself and praying with me and for me and keeping me encouraged as I moved out of my comfort zone and began my transition from simply existing to actually living.

Roniquia Nicholas there are not enough words to express my love and gratitude for each of you. Thank you for helping me go through my process and to write my journey. Thank you for your brutally honest opinions even when I didn't want it, thank you for being persistent when I was slacking, and thank you for allowing me to love, laugh, and lean on you.

Thank you to all my family and friends for your unconditional love and support.

A Hidden Heart is the internal race to freedom between mind and heart and the battles that lye in between. There are some of the poems and journals created while on the journey of putting the pieces back together again.

Secret Contents...

1. Spiritually Drowning 11
2. Stick Together 13
3. Church Hurt 15
4. What The? 17
5. Faith 18
6. Speak Life 20
7. Hidden Truth 22
8. Truth Moment 24
9. Their Blood on Your Hands 26
10. Closest Thing to Jesus 28
11. Unspoken Dreams 30
12. Didn't Know My Own Strength 31
13. I Hate My Body 34
14. Why I Hate My Body 36
15. Dead Inside 42
16. Lost 44
17. An Empty Life 47
18. Suicide 49
19. Live Today 51
20. Live 53
21. Better Than This 55
22. 360 Days 56
23. Mirror Me 58

24.	Big Dreams Then None	60
25.	I Trusted You	62
26.	Just Trust Me	63
27.	Confused	65
28.	Whispering Dreams	70
29.	Gone for Real	71
30.	You Are Not Alone	73
31.	You Can Run but You Can't Hide	75
32.	Though I Believe	78
33.	The Fight	80
34.	Watchful Words	82
35.	Going Back	83
36.	Big Girl Blues	84
37.	Transparency	86
38.	Streams of Consciousness	88
39.	Love me	93
40.	Worth	95
41.	I Write	98
42.	Write Today	99
43.	God or Nothing	102
44.	The Lesson	104
Note from the author		108
About the author		110

Spiritually Drowning

CALLING ALL SAINTS
CALLING ALL SAINTS
CALLING ALL SAINTS
This is a 911 alter call
from the emergency soul saving network
And we're not calling the super saved
But those of you that can really make a difference
No hindrances
Because we have a child that is spiritually drowning
And no offense but this ain't a time
where the self-righteous can help this
Cause see right now, right now
My soul's too weak for the fronting, fake Christians
that are only saved on Sunday
And I can't wait not another day
See, with every passing moment my soul is slowly dying
I am Spiritually Drowning
Can't even write a happy poem
Because my soul's in need of a healing
For I am spiritually drowning
But I don't think ya'll understand me
I said I AM SPIRITUALLY DROWNING
My soul is slowly dying and
I'm crying out for help in a room full of saints
where no one is listening
No one will reach out to me, I'm on my knees,
the center of attention,
ALL... EYES... ON... ME...
And They're Pointing...
They're Laughing...
They're... Stealing... My... Oxygen...
And... Leaving... Me... Drowning...
Church hurt has painted itself a mirage

and descended upon my soul a whole new meaning
And GOD...
I've tried to see things objectively
I've placed myself in their situations,
Walked a mile in their shoes,
and embraced their stories
as if they were my own
Tried to breathe freedom but they're making
my mental anguish a home for their comfort zone
And God, GOD
you can't even come a midst because
your Sunday worshipers are too busy
crucifying my sins with their judgment
I CAN'T TAKE IT
Lord I love you, but the hurt, the hurt it's taking its toll
I need help
I need healing to exceed life's potential promises
I need H.E.L.P help
I need a **H**ealing to **E**xceed **L**ife's **P**otential **P**romises
And I didn't rehearse this
I can't regurgitate it and recite it like Sunday morning devotion
The words I speak are my pains in motion
CAUSE SEE I'M DROWNING
And God please don't restore me but make me whole for I've
always been incomplete
And I'm on my last strand of sanity
desperately reaching out to save this drowning soul in need
This is a prayer I don't have strength enough to repeat
So, if I die today at least have enough sympathy
to float off your high horse and say a single prayer for my family
After all it's not like someone effortlessly attempted
to reach out and help me
Cause see it was the saints that left my soul
SPIRITUALLY DROWNING....

"Stick Together"

I can't help but wondering if all church folks with a title stick together or something. Is it like some unwritten code that right or wrong they defend each other? I respected her and her position. So, I believed her when she told me that the reason I was attracting so much of the wrong kind of attention was because of how I dressed. What she didn't tell me was that no matter what I wore I'd attract the same attention. She told me I was responsible for him taking a total disregard to me yelling, "NO... STOP..." He attempted to take from me everything he wanted that I wasn't willing to give, but because he was a minister it was ok. I couldn't even get people to pray for me without having to go in depth with explaining what was wrong and why I needed someone to pray for me.

They were in leadership roles. Why couldn't they just do a general prayer for me? I don't understand it but now it doesn't even matter anymore. The very ones in leadership that I thought were going to help me blamed me. They told me it was something in me that caused it. It was a spirit I was carrying. How can anyone carry a spirit that allows their words to mean nothing? What kind of spirit can a person carry that says, "oh yes take my innocence, take my purity"? I needed for someone to help me pray that spirit away. I lacked the knowledge and understanding of what a predator really was. At the time, I didn't know they actually existed and I was surrounded by a multitude of them.

All I knew was this was the route I was supposed to take to get closer to Jesus. I wanted a better relationship with Him and church was where I had to go to get that. I needed someone to show me how to get to the place I wanted to be in God. So, I did what I was taught to do. I knew that when you prayed, you were supposed to talk to God just like you talk to the people around you. So, I did that, but I didn't think He could hear me. I didn't think He really knew who I was because so much was happening around me and it hurt. I just wanted them to pray for me. I can't trust them. I tried to, and they made a mockery of me. Preached about the sins I caused others to commit. Laughed at my misery. Took pride in my pain but I still went to church every time the doors opened trying to find my way to Jesus. I could be sitting in the midst of everyone at church and still felt like the loneliest person in the world. I just wanted somebody to pray for me. Yet no matter what happened I had to believe that things would get better. They had to.

Church Hurt

Opposites attracted as a child but now I'm grown
Done put away childish things and
about three words away from being long gone
See there's too many fly by night Christians
wanting a microwave blessing
Wolves in sheep's clothing just here for the
show and tell portion of impressing
Then there's you... You proclaim to do a new thang
but where's your victory?
You're living double lives
Feeding into the controversy of Christianity
Covering spiritual graves with missing names
Just to create a shift in the blame
An in essence the story line still remains the same
Cause see though your words don't judge me
your actions do
So let ye who goes without sin cast the first stone
Where does the perfection lie at in you?
And just because I sin don't mean that I ain't saved
And just because I'm saved don't mean that I won't sin
See from the head of the church on down
we all got struggles we fight to win
And when it's all said and done
the truth proves to be self-evident
That through the hypocrisy flowing from your lips
The heart speaks what's most relevant
Quoting prophelying scriptorials
that's got the beginners on their way back home
Casting out more souls than you bring in
due to the artificial love you've continuously shown
Meanwhile back stabbing and backbiting
have become your right of passage
As the blood of souls

drenches your hand by the masses
Teaching the weak there's no difference
between the streets and the church
Igniting the flames that burden
the heart with its hurts
So I ask that you realize it's time out
for being punks with Christ
Cause that ain't what you were called to
God didn't sacrifice His only son
for fear and defeat to consume you
Cause see the steps of a good man
are ordered by the Lord
It's time you put on your full armor
and pick up your swords
And if the games you play
are gaining victory in your life
Then you need to find out who you've
really been serving throughout your life
As for me, know that no weapons you form
can ever consume me
Because despite what you say
I know who I am and what I'm destined to be
So, for all of you under the sound of my voice
I now leave you in my memory
Knowing...
That before the foundations of the Earth
I was formed in my mother's womb
Open mindedly creating lyrics
that will forever be inscribed
on the walls of even my descendant's tombs.

"What's The?"

No matter what is happening around me or what I see, I think I just woke up one day and realized that there has to be more to Jesus... to church... than sex, lies, backstabbing, scandals, affairs, bruises, scars, hurt, pain, sorrow, deceit, and misery. What's the purpose of going to church if you're going to have to fight the saints just like you fight the sinners when you leave back out the doors of the church house? What's the purpose of going to church if the people inside of it aren't willing to help you heal from your hurt but, willing to add to it? How can we be effective Christians if we never care about anyone but ourselves? How can new believers be saved if Christians aren't willing to get off the pew and meet people right where they are? Meet them in the depths of their pain in order to lead them back to Jesus? What part of us looks like Jesus? How do you explain to the beginners in Christ the difference between Jesus and the devil when the devil they see stares them in the face every day? The church has so much corruption in it that the people are more lost coming inside the building than they were living out on the street? What do you say to them?

I woke up and realized there had to be another way to Jesus than what I see. I didn't know what it was, but I knew I was going to find it by any means necessary. I didn't even know why I needed to find it so bad but I just felt like I had to. I didn't know how many people I'd piss off or have to fight along the way. I wanted more... I needed more than what I was surrounded by. I woke up one day and I knew one thing... that as long as I held on to even just a tiny bit of faith I could get out from where I was. I realized that I was more than what people said about me. I was more than what they did to me and there had to be more to life... to God... to being a Christian than heartache. I believed that one day someone would reach me and I would reach back and reach out to someone else. I realized that even though I didn't know my purpose or the purpose of anything happening around me. I knew that even though sticks and stones could break my bones and the words of people could try to destroy me but, I would survive no matter what. I wouldn't give anyone the satisfaction in watching me die slowly.

Faith

Every day I tried to be someone else
Cause I hated what I saw when I looked at myself
I believed the words my examples fed me
And maybe some of you have heard them too
Things like...
You're stupid, you're ignorant, you're fat, you're ugly
They were role models whose phrases stayed with me
And every so often I can still hear their words echoing
Then God took my mama but wouldn't take me
I was only 14 and still needed training
Maybe if I would have worked a little harder
she'd still be living
I always blamed me for her leaving
And there was no one around
to give me a better understanding
See at the time
I wasn't close to my daddy
And though he did the best he could
I was a mama's girl
And a man raising girls ain't easy
And in my book God didn't really exist
Because If he did I wouldn't have so many anointed little finger
tips trying to rob me of my innocence
They prayed scriptures in me in the morning
but hurt me at night
What was I to believe?
Pastors he supposedly called to train up a child
in the way that they should go
But when I got old I still departed from thee
Not just God but my family
I held secrets that stalked me in my memories
All my life church has planted most of my hurting seeds
The lies, rumors, and back stabbing stares
mounted walls in me that grew evenly

Love and trust posted signs on my heart and read vacancy
And in the midst of my most suicidal storms
is when I first heard him whispering
God gently called... saying
"Everybody that calls themselves anointed
aren't appointed by me
Your trials are your testimonies
Stories that encourage those stranded
where you used to be
See I've never left you nor forsaken you,
from the womb I set you on the course for your destiny
I know your limitations and though you're
weeping now your joy comes in the morning
I'll never put more on you than you can bare
Your storms are only temporary
And when I came for your mama it was her time
And you weren't ready; you weren't to blame
You were nowhere near the completion of your ministry
And during those times when you were too weak to stand I
Carried you along your journey
So now comes the time to mend the gap
between you and me
Let me in to begin your healing,
I love you and I'm knocking
Faith is the substance of things hoped for and
the evidence of things not seen
I've continuously proven myself to you,
but into your life you still speak negativity
I force myself on no one,
life and death are spoken through the power of the tongue
Out of your mouth you speak what
your ears will hear, your
Mind will think, and your heart will receive
And I can only accept what you choose to believe."

"Speak Life"

Today I asked myself these questions: What do you want out of life? What do you want to achieve? Are you letting your pain overcome your destiny? Do you know what your destiny is? How do you operate in your fullest potential? Do you know or even recognize the potential you have? I couldn't answer all the questions I asked but in trying to answer I realized one thing. My words contained power. I think the reason so much happened... the reason I went through so much hurt is because long before I realized my words had power, someone else knew it and set out to shatter that part of me. Sometimes we have to try to make the best out of what life throws at us. It's not always easy, especially when it seems like the world is against you. Even in those most difficult moments, you still have to find a way to speak life to yourself and over your situation.

No matter how hard it gets (and there will be times when it gets real hard), you have to stay focused and know that the storm won't last forever. You have to speak life. Remembering to speak life when you're filled with so much heartache and pain can be one of the most difficult things to do in life. Especially in those moments where all you want to do is die and the urge to die is so bad it consumes you. It's all you think about and breathe in. Don't give up. Out of your mouth you speak what your ears will hear and your heart will receive. What you put out there is what you'll get back. Keep speaking life to your situation and life will get better. I can say this because I know it to be true. I've been in places in my life that I wouldn't wish upon my worst enemy. I even lived through the death of my mother.

My mama was my life line and now she's gone. I felt like I was lacking. I'm empty. I feel so hollow inside and it hurts. Some days are harder to breathe than others. There's so much pain. She left me. I felt like I was the one to blame. I felt like I was the reason that she's dead. I felt like maybe I could've worked harder at taking care of her so she would've lived. I wonder if she knows how much I loved her and how helpless I felt trying to care for her. I wish I could go back in time and do some things differently. I wish I could talk to her. I wish I could ask her questions about my body and about life. There's so much I don't know and people make fun of me for not knowing so I don't say anything. I don't know who's meaner... the adults or my peers.

As I got older I realized adults and peers are equal in the meanness they share. I often wonder who I'm supposed to talk to, confide in and learn from. Even now I still wonder. She was my life line and I felt like once she left I spent years dying a slow and painful death from the inside out. I was rotting alone among a multitude of people. People pretended to care at first but that didn't last long. There was so much chaos and confusion all over the place the moment they pronounced her dead. But before they said it I knew it. I knew when I looked at her face she was gone. I walked into our living room looking for my game, and found my mother on the living room floor dead.

My world changed forever. From that moment on I looked to people to fill the void and the emptiness I felt on the inside. Eventually I learned to stop looking at people to fill something in me that they didn't have the ability to do. People couldn't complete me. Just like they couldn't destroy me but they tried and I almost allowed them to do it. We possess the power to speak life and death over ourselves no matter what anybody else says or does. I realized that I am a lot bigger than any tragedy or trial I go through. I learned to speak life to myself no matter what it looks like, and trust and believe that at the end of the day everything will be ok. My words have power and I'm learning that as I live I have power too. I realized that when you speak your words flow out of your mouth, back into your ear, up to your mind and then back down into your heart. Your heart then holds on to it and stores it away for safe keeping. What you speak is what you deposit in.

Hidden Truths

I spent most of my life out casted
feeling like the ugly ducking
Too busy pleasing people and caught
up in what they said to me
I had no individual identity
My reflection revealed a variety of images
shaped by their opinions
Believing everything they told me
That I'd never amount to anything
I looked too different to be seen
As it messed with my understanding
I remembered mama once telling me
Don't' believe everything people said to me
They'd play on my insecurities
To destroy my reality
And there's no real victory in evil dwellings
But because I found mama dead on the
living room floor when I was 14
I needed fulfillment to replace being empty
So if you could imagine it then I've got the story
I needed someone to love me and I was willing
to gain that by any means necessary
Now I fight daily against poisonous obscenities
shot out to shatter my destiny
By the very ones I begged to touch and agree

They'd rather use my past against me
When church has held my firsts of everything
It's where I was trained to sin professionally
Now they're too busy judging and labeling me
To intercede against these demons I'm fighting
Said do what you do when I gave up my body
for carnal things

Sold my soul to the devil for friendships
that weren't worth having
And though we all came from a
religious teaching
We picked and chose the scriptures
worth keeping
See I dealt with too many church folks
and not enough for real Christians
But I've got one word for you.... DELIVERENCE!!!!!!

"Truth Moment"

It seems like it's always the people closest to you that will hurt you the most. Yet since those closest to me were the ones that were supposed to love me the most, I believed everything they told me. I clung to the words they spoke as if they only spoke the truth. I had no opinion of my own. My identity was built upon what other people told me I was and how they taught me to be. Though I could think for myself and determine what was right and wrong, sometimes it took me a little longer to figure out that the things they were portraying as right were actually wrong. The consequences behind going against the grain were sometimes so severe that even if you did know what was right, you went along with it because pretending was a whole lot easier both emotionally and physically than dealing with the consequences.

The only problem with that is the more you block out the warnings or that feeling you get on the inside telling you not to follow the crowd, the worse things get for you. The more I followed what I was told and taught instead of listening to my instincts, the harder it became to look at myself in the mirror. The easier it became for people to point out all the things I did wrong when I was trying to do right. In trying to fill the emptiness I had on the inside of me I ended up around a lot of pretenders. They pretended to pray when they were actually preying. They pretended to have my best interests at heart when I was actually being manipulated and used. They talked about me and lied on me, beat me, stabbed me, cut me physically and wounded me spiritually.

When I'd want someone to pray with me... pray that I could find my way out of the situations I got in, following behind the church folks, I was ridiculed because of my past as if they didn't have one. The very ones who were supposed to pray with me were the first ones to shun me. How come the same God that saved them couldn't save me? I don't understand these people. You pray, worship, speak in tongues but push away the very ones you're supposed to minister to. So, if salvation could be measured, how saved are you? In my opinion your title can't save you or anyone else. So, what's the point in having a title if there's no substance behind it? Nothing about your title makes me want to know God. I might not know much but I do know that you can't serve God with a disobedient spirit doing anything you want to.

What makes you so different from me that you can fall short and go to heaven and I can't because of my past? We're both God's children. Why is it that He could deliver you but my sins are so bad that the same God that delivered you can't deliver me too? Well here's what I know now... I don't know much but I've come to realize that there is a difference between church folks and for real Christians. You can't base your walk with Christ on other people. Despite what you see happening around you, no matter what you got involved in in your life, God has the ability to pull you out of anything. The process isn't going to be easy though. So while you're fighting to change, keep this in mind... You've got to tell yourself "I'm not staying like this, I can't stay this way any longer, you will not have your way, I'm fighting my way out of this situation." You can't live in God's will with one foot in and one foot out. Don't let people stop you from changing, growing, or knowing God.

Their Blood on Your Hands

Four pews back she watched him coming
Sliding in and quoting the words he spoke on Sunday morning
But in a different context
So she absorbed her essence in his scriptures of I love you's and just trust me's
Accented with promise rings of secret foreverness
Never to be shared beyond the shadows she kept creeping
And pretending in hopes that one day his promises would be reality
Cause see he was the closest thing she ever had to Jesus and she just wanted to know him better
So she aborted her soul for his moans and cries
While spiritually she died
For what he called a touch of thee anointing
Sworn to secrecy
Forbidden to say anything
Because to speak of her experiences speaks ill against the ministry
So to her grave she takes the pulpits painted portrait of salvation on her knees
All the while questioning the difference between the church and the streets
Cause see he was the closest thing she ever had to Jesus and she just wanted to know him better
But instead she was biblically pimped out by a
self-proclaimed teacher
As Christians the blood shed of beginners is
our responsibility
Somebody's got to intercede
Somebody's got to be accountable for the false seeds planted on the inexperienced, weak, & those gullibly desiring to merely believe
For most of them our lives is the only Bible they'll ever read
And for those too wounded to reach these doors you can't save from the pews of the ministry

Who will pray for the lost if the ones that's supposed to be there feeds their souls with so much hypocrisy
Painting this portrait of her Christian experiences that left her lying exposed, unprotected, damaged, and dying
And so many saints are standing by doing nothing
Who will save the lost and inflicted if the church is corrupting more lives than its redeeming
She's shattered and destroyed but she kept attending all the while praying
Crying out for FOR REAL FOR REAL Christians to help her find **HIM**
But until then she unknowingly keeps settling for these hypocritical preachers spreading false teaching of who Jesus really is
Because see he was the closest thing she ever had to Jesus AND she just wanted to know HIM better

"Closest Thing to Jesus"

Coming into this Christian journey I entered in under false pretenses. Though I wasn't sure quite what to expect, I had my own interpretation of what I thought being saved was going to be like. I thought it was going to be an easy walk and I trusted everybody I was around because of their title and the spiritual position they appeared to be in. I didn't know coming in that I had just gotten myself tangled up in another layer of a big spider web that was extremely hard to get out of. The things I saw, did, experienced, and learned took me down roads I couldn't ever see anyone on. Being on it though gave me the opportunity to look at things from an entirely different perspective. I realize just how the people in this generation are nothing like the type that existed when my parents were coming up. Just like the people that will exist after my generation will grow up nothing like my generation did. So what's my point in saying that?

My point is that, as Christians, the things that worked to draw people to Christ when our parents were children are not the same tactics that will work when trying to bring in someone in my generation or younger than me. The pretenders, the wolves in sheep's clothing are a lot better today than they were decades ago. So, it's gonna take some different skills and techniques to reach people because in the eyes of the unsaved all Christians have been roped into the same ball of fakeness. You're guilty by association already and you can't save and deliver people who you can't relate to. And you sure can't help anyone sitting on the pew doing nothing, watching them go through and don't even offer them a prayer, let alone some assistance. You don't have to give them the world but at least give them a little compassion. A scripture to meditate on, some friendly advice, the channels they can go down to get out of where they are.... SOMETHING.... Something is always better than nothing at all.

On this road I also realized the influence I had over other people. I had people around me that followed me down the roads I went down just because it was me going down them. Then they blamed me for the hell they went through when they were on those roads. I felt bad. I felt guilty. Even though it was never my intent to go to the places I did. I was trying to be a good friend. I was trying to find my way to Jesus and in the midst I trusted the wrong people. I couldn't tell the difference between those pretending to live for Christ and those that actually were until it was too late. As a result, this past week has been one for the records. I can't believe everything I found out. As I began to encounter a few for real for real Christians, I started to learn the difference between who they were and who I was with.

    I began to understand that the things they were doing weren't right and I had no choice but to totally let go and surrender to God. Sometimes it seems like being saved is just too hard for me, but I'm going to try it. I'm saying I tried everything else. It seems like I know so much of the wrong stuff that trying to do what I'm supposed to do just don't feel right. It feels so wrong. I feel so unworthy. Nevertheless, I'm going to keep trying till I get it right and in the meantime, I've got to emotionally disconnect myself and move on. Cause Lord knows these folks right here are wilder than a goose and I can't roll with them no more.

    If I'm ever gonna prosper in anything in life, with everything that's been taking place, I realize now before I died in the guilt behind all this mess I was wrapped up in, God had to remove the veil and show me the real deal so that I could fully start all over again. I couldn't afford to go backwards and I had no reason to feel guilty. Yes, as a Christian, for some you are the only Bible they'll ever read. But, when you are a beginner yourself, five days into your journey, you cannot try to lead anybody or be a light for anyone else. You're too fresh out of the womb to stand on your own. You've got to get your life together first. I followed, thinking I was being led in the right direction. I didn't tell anyone else to follow me and when I realized the road I was on was the wrong one I fought to get off of it. I told the people who followed me on it to get off too. They didn't. So, the blood of others would not be spilled on my hands because of the bad decisions or unwise choices they decided to make. IT'S NOT MY FAULT!

Unspoken Dreams

For years I was my only encouragement....
My own comfort in a time of need
My only wisdom – Right or wrong
It was the lessons from my trials that
became my greatest lead
I played the role of my security
to my insecurities and fears
Held my head high, swallowed hard,
and shielded all my tears
I was my own back bone....
Strength when times got rough
Love in the midnight hour....
Comfort when times got tough
Protected my heart from life's defeats
I built barriers you later discovered
only kept me weak
You entered my thoughts and were exquisitely
created into my existence
Uniquely formed to defy all boundaries
not limited by life's hindrances
Elegantly designed as a childhood dream
I could never share
You were the unimaginable finding success by any means
Gracefully outlined with a glow of anointing divinely seen
You poured loves wisdom from your eyes
through the windows of your soul
Completed life's incompletions so the broken
can be made whole
Brought life back to my lyrics that
dwindled away with the unseen
You descended from my vision
as my faiths unspoken dream.

"Didn't Know My Own Strength"

The only thing I was ever really consistent at was being inconsistent. I didn't know how strong I really was until I was put in a position where I had absolutely nothing and no one to rely on but me. I didn't know what kind of faith I had until all I could do was pray. I had nothing and was barely putting a roof over my head. When I say nothing, I mean absolutely nothing. I didn't even have 35 cents to buy myself a pack of gum. The freezer, fridge, and cabinets were all empty. Do you know what it feels like to be so hungry that you're dizzy and praying that somebody would come by and bring you some food or take you out to eat? But when they do you eat just enough to calm the hunger pains but you want left overs so you can eat again tomorrow. Have you ever been in a place so low in your life that all you could do was ask strangers for help and pray someone came through?

I had no job, no food, no money, failing health, car not running, and a list of problems as long as my arm. Almost everybody that stood in my corner walked away. When I thought I had hit rock bottom and couldn't dive any deeper, everything got worse. I didn't get in this position by choice. I got here by circumstances that were beyond my control. When I felt like I had it all and was sitting on top of the world, I had an abundance of people around me. But when I had nothing, the amount of friends I had dwindled down to almost nothing. I was sick and I was hurt but no matter how bad things looked on the outside and no matter how much pain I was in on the inside, I couldn't give up. My spirit wouldn't die even when my body acted like it was trying to. It was at that moment that I realized just how strong I really was.

Every day I prayed because it was all that I could do to stay sane in the moment. I learned to stop worrying about things that I couldn't control and to let the pieces fall where they may. I wasn't in a position where I could control anything happening around me. I had to find the lesson in that moment and keep going. I didn't think I had much of a spiritual life but I actually had more in me than I knew. When the doctors gave up on me, said there was nothing left that they could do and told me to call my family, I told them God's got the final say and it ain't over. I walked out of the hospital a week later only to get home and have an eviction notice taped to my door. I hadn't worked in two months and should've been evicted a long time ago because I was living pay check to pay check. No check, no rent money. I said a prayer and went to the leasing office.

While I was in the hospital they switched managers. I walked in and introduced myself to the new manager. We sat in her office and I told her my situation. She said "even though you should've been gone I'll do everything I can to help you out. I'll come check on you too." I said "if you come in and I'm not there, I didn't move. I'm probably back in the hospital. So, don't put my stuff out thinking I'm gone". She said ok. I went in with weekly updates on my situation and if she didn't see me she'd send someone by to make sure I wasn't passed out in my apartment. She said she was amazed that I could be going through all that and still be in such good spirits. I told her it was nobody but God that had me still going. She handed me a list of different places to contact to see if any of them could assist me with rent and bills. She told me not to worry about anything as far as living was concerned and sent me on my way to go rest.

When the cabinets were completely empty and the lights were hours away from being disconnected, I went to apply for a program where they could pay my lights. When I got there I was the only black person in the building and the people were rude. They talked down to me as if I was nothing. I wanted to run. I was already hurting, sick, and now humiliated. But in the midst of the situation I started to pray that God would help me to hold my tongue and control my attitude. Because no matter how low they made me feel, at the end of the day I needed help. I needed them to help me. There was nowhere else to go and I was racing the clock to keep from being in the dark. I let them say all they were gonna say and when it was my turn to account for myself I began to tell my story. How I ended up in this state and why I would never be in this position again. They cried for me even though I didn't shed a tear. The people in the room with me cried so hard they went and got other workers in the building to come hear my story.

By the time I finished speaking one woman asked me... "well how do you know that your situation is only temporary and how are you gonna get through?" I said "because I know God didn't bring me this far in my life to abandon me now. I know that even though things look mighty bad right now, storms are only temporary. No storm lasts forever when you know Jesus." Not only did they pay my electric bill in full but they put a credit on my bill for the next month. They also gave me three extra-large bags of food that filled up my cabinets, freezer, and fridge. I thanked and praised God all the way home. I knew it was nobody but God.

By the time I returned home my phone was ringing with a job offer for a job I didn't apply for, paying more money than the one I lost. Won't HE Do IT 😊 I went to see the location, interviewed and was hired all in a two week period. In a month's time I was not only able to get caught up on the rent from the previous three months but get ahead and be in a position to help someone else. When you are under pressure, things begin to come out of you that you didn't even know was in you to say. That's how my faith kicked in one day. I didn't even know how much word I actually had rooted on the inside of me. Until I was sitting at rock bottom, looking up encouraging myself not to give up, laying dying and defeated... But to keep going and trust and believe God that things were going to get better because faith was the only thing I had to myself at the time. See you've got to learn how to cry out to God during the battle while you still have a chance of winning. Not once the battle is over and you're crying because you have so many scars, cuts, and bruises. Sometimes God will remove everybody and everything from around you that is hindering you from getting closer to him, just so He can get your attention and have enough room to show you who He really is. If you ever want to know what God can do for you, try Him and have enough patience to wait on Him to show up for you.

I Hate My Body

I need to be free
Trapped within my mind and hating what I see
So through the ink of my pen flows my sanity
It's hard for me.....
Looking back on the days of simply being happy
Going through trials but knowing they were only temporary
Until now......
Six months and counting, still bleeding, trying to look ahead but all I see is red rivers flowing, pains aching, limited mobility, my sanity slipping, and doctors unable to do anything
But say "your only option now is a hysterectomy"
I scream GOD I HATE MY BODY

See nobody knows the inadequacies I feel but me
My friends stopped listening, my reality was
unimaginably too hard for them to see
Months of pushing painful clots that felt like semi's passing
Each month hundreds of dollars spent, borrowed, and lent
Just so I can stay ahead of misery
I go through this... NOT YOU..... ME.....
And despite my own situation I was there when you
needed me but all of you left me with nothing
Yet you have the nerve to ask me why I'm bitter and angry
Come hold me, hold my hand and let me know
all this is worth me living
Every day's a struggle and I'm held in captivity
The corners of my dark walls are closing in on me
I'm suffocating and you're watching
My life is changing, my faith depleting,
trying to stay strong but my grip is slipping
I try to pray but blindsided by my rage all I can manage to say is
GOD..... I HATE MY BODY
Tired of being compared to the woman
with the issue of blood

that I made it to the hem of his garment
and it came back again
Only this time it won't end
And I'm sick of hearing it's a great testimony
cause when I tell it the saints
throw monetary seeds towards
the purchase of the materials
used to "catch the leak"
Each pain keeps me counting, rivers flowing,
shedding pieces of my sanity,
in the solitude and hatred of my body

"Why I Hate My Body"

I spent the last 9 years as a lab rat because my body was just as dysfunctional as my life. Losing my baby was a blessing and a curse. It was a curse because I'll never get to have one but it was a blessing because in losing her, the doctors found out I had other issues with my body. First it was irregular cycles (a normal period for me would last between 14 and 31 days). Even after losing her and having a DNC it only stopped the bleeding for a few days. I still bled for months after that. I also had polyps in my gall bladder which where cancerous so I had surgery and had my gall bladder removed. Once I healed from the surgery my bleeding went from 14-31 days to 2-6 months. Then it went from 2-6 months to 6 months – 1 year and a half.

Yes, you just read that right. I would bleed for a year and a half at a time. It would then stop for a week or two depending on the meds, then start right back up again. It didn't miss a blow or a beat. I was spending $40-50.00 a week on pads. The bleeding would be extremely heavy the entire time. Eventually I had to upgrade to adult diapers. I was so humiliated. I felt like people could see them through my clothes. I went to doctor after doctor and specialist after specialist. Nobody could help me. I was miserable and welcomed the weeks that I would have a break. All the doctors did was provide me more and more meds that weren't helping. I spent years on 14 medications.

Most of the meds they gave me made me extremely sick... even the birth controls. I had medications to help with the side effects of the original medications. During the first time I bled for a year and a half I saw about 10 different doctors. One told me it was all in my head. I told him he needed to tell me where the damn shut off valve was because this has gotten absolutely ridiculous. Another doctor told me in her history of being a physician she had never seen a case like mine and she didn't know what to do. Then she went and pulled out the thickest book I've ever seen. She went through it and pointed out all the things it could've possibly been. I respected her for trying and respected her honesty. She was my last hope... so I thought. Two months later I ended up in the hospital with one pint of blood left running through my whole body.

That was the first of many more times this would happen. The first time, I was in too much pain and feeling too sick to be scared about anything. The longer these bleeding sessions would last the more pain I was in. I no longer had a regular flow. It was just extra-large clots which you and I both know hurt like hell coming out. Normally by the third one I've ruined everything I was wearing. I think it would've been easier to deal with one or the other. I think I could've handled the pain or the bleeding but the combination of the two was driving me insane. I spent many days crying and crawling up the wall in pain. Most days it felt like I was trying to give birth to a semi-truck.

Being hospitalized because the pain levels were so high... I never knew there were pain meds stronger than morphine but, when they gave it to me I could feel it slowly burning and moving through my body. On a scale of 1-10 my normal pain levels would be between 11-15. At one point I was having black outs and passing out all over the place. It's hard dealing with a lot of medical issues and still walking around every day pretending like you're normal because you're all you've got to depend on.

As if I needed to add on anything else. I could be in the middle of talking to someone and pass out. The first time it happened and I woke up on the ground I was so scared. I remember passing out and people would look at me like I was crazy. My "friend" would tell them "oh don't worry about her she'll come to in a little while. It's alright she does this all the time". They were so used to it that they were no longer concerned about it. So, the people watching me began to lose their concern and proceed to walk around me.

In the midst of all these physical problems I was still getting up going to school every day and working, all the while praying I didn't fall out or mess up my clothes. I didn't have anybody to take care of me. If I didn't work I didn't eat and my bills didn't get paid. The bill collectors didn't care nothing about how I felt or what I was going through. I felt like didn't nobody else in my life care either. My eyes had started to look sunken in and I was beyond exhausted. But I got up and pulled myself together and went to school anyway. I made it to school and tried to do my final presentation but could barely stand. They told me to go to the hospital. I didn't feel the need because they were never able to do anything.

So, I left and went home to freshen up instead. I went home and laid down but I kept hearing... "don't close your eyes". My eyes kept closing... "don't close your eyes". I laid there and tried to pull myself back up. As I struggled to get up I told God... "God I need your help. I want to go to sleep and I have no more energy left to keep going." All of a sudden I had a little more strength. When I got up out of the bed and looked back, the bed was covered in blood. I cleaned myself up and drove to the hospital. When I got there they started running tests and the doctor came in and said... "well I can't help you but I'll do my best to make you comfortable." I told him to go ahead.

That's more than anybody else has been able to do. So, he began to go to work. Nurses started running in and out. Each one started to look more panicked than the one before. The doctor came back in looking scared. He said your tests show that you have one pint of blood left running through your entire body. Medically, you are already dead. There is no explanation as to why you are even conscious and able to communicate right now. I said I know why. He said why. I said "because God told me not to close my eyes when I wanted to go to sleep."

He said, "we are going to need to admit you right away and pump blood back into your body but it doesn't look good for you". I called my dad and he came right away. The doctor told him they were going to make me as comfortable as possible but they didn't think I was going to make it through the night. He said to call all our family so they could say their goodbyes. Ha! The devil is a lie. As fast as they pumped the blood in it came right out the other end. They called the Chief OBGYN at home and had her come in because they didn't know what to do. She came in and looked at my file and kept talking to me the whole time.

She wasn't quite sure what to do exactly but she reassured me she too would do the best she could. I left the hospital a couple of days later. That was the first time. I had many more of these experiences that followed over the next two years. They started to come more and more frequently. Between the asthma attacks, the constant pain and the continuous bleeding, most days felt like I was losing my mind and I prayed to die. My body felt like I was dying a slow death. I was utterly miserable and so many people walked away from me because of my health and no longer wanted to hear about what I was going through.

When you are in a house alone and miserable, your mind becomes an easy playground for the devil to get in. There've been some days where the silence of my house and the magnitude of my pain left me trapped inside my own head with no escape. Going through that much does something to you. Then add hurt on top of it all. I was betrayed by one of the closest people to me and it hurt me to my core but, there was no time to focus on that. I had more pressing situations at hand. I was fighting to live.

I never knew how much our physical situations play a part in our health situations until I went through. As a result of my medical situation, all the falling out at work and missing so many days, I also lost yet another job. My life was spiraling out of control more rapidly than I could've ever imagined. Rent was going to be due soon. I ended up back in the hospital again and unemployment wasn't going to kick in any time soon. I called everybody I could think of and nobody could help me. In between the hospital stays I was going to the library filling out job applications as much as possible. When your back is against the wall and you're trapped with nowhere to go and you can't even depend on your own body to work in your favor, it puts you in a real bad place. Especially mentally but, it also shows you that God is real and allows you to depend solely on Him and watch Him move. Here's how...

I'd be shaking because I was in so much pain and was trying to function through it. But the way my body felt, there was no way on Earth I could've gotten through all that operating in my own will. I needed God's help to keep moving. People talked to me as if I was lower than dirt for needing them until I explained why I was in the state that I was in. Then they helped. See God can use anybody to help you in the midst of the storm. I took life one moment at a time because anything more than the moment was too much for me to handle. Sometimes those moments even seemed too great. I also started seeing a specialist that I was recommended to.

He looked at my medical record over the previous nine years and said, "The doctors you've been dealing with didn't know what they were doing because this should never have gone on this long. I want to try a few different options and if they don't work you're going to have to have a hysterectomy. Do you mind if I try a few things first?" I said "no I've been a guinea pig for everybody else. I might as well be one for you too." He tried all his options and when none of them worked he said, "unfortunately I've exhausted all my resources and it's either have the hysterectomy or die." Since I'm writing this you can tell I chose the latter of the two. I knew what I had to do and I was ok with that. Considering everything I had been going through, especially in the last 2 years of my 9-year trial, I still didn't really understand the emotional weight that would come behind making this decision. I was ready for what I was expecting, not for what happened after. I still feel so inadequate as a woman. But I'm sitting here thinking back to the places God has brought me from and the things he brought me through. I could've been taken out so many times. BUT GOD.......

My arm stretched up I'm reaching
And grabbing nothing
Giving up seemed so easy
These challenges feel bigger than me
But I encourage myself to keep fighting
Cause greater is He that is in me
And though I know the word don't get it twisted
THIS WALK AIN'T EASY
And though I believe I pray constantly for
God to help my unbelief
It gets hard to keep encouraging yourself when

there's so much that is discouraging
When the continuous pain in my body
knocks the wind out of me
And I keep praying for a healing but I see nothing
And though my body's wrecked with pain
I keep pushing forcing a smile
and KEEP FIGHTING........

Dead Inside

She died in me
She... Died... In... Me
But for every day that she lived she was a part of me
Until I killed her....
The inadequacies of my body
took from me a childhood dream of being a mommy
My body conducted its own abortion
without me consenting
In that moment I felt like an epic failure
worthlessly living
So throughout the years I've learned to cope with things
that will never be for me what is most women's reality
Pregnancy.......
But it's the one I continuously see
And with each friend announcing theirs,
excitement mixed with envy
Because my announcement
will never be made

Instead of having another opportunity
I had to choose between giving birth and living
And well I chose me
I sacrificed your existence so I could be totally free
of a 9-year uphill battle that gave my misery
and abundance of company without me
And though the decision was somewhat easy
I forced myself to believe that there wouldn't be
an emotional attachment behind the decision
I was making
I wanted to live but living ain't easy when
your emotions are weighing heavy

So I stuff them in a suitcase that I keep
buried on the inside of me
With all the other wounds I slapped band aids
on and hid away for no one to see
In the moment she died inside me
I felt ashamed, embarrassed, and empty
So I stuffed those too and kept on living
But not once did I ever forget her existing
She was supposed to be my beginning of many
But my body had a different reality
and instead she died in me

"Lost"

Yesterday was supposed to be special. It was Mother's Day. I was so excited to see it coming but it's funny how things never go according to how I plan them. It was awful. I got up cramping and praying my monthly didn't show up early. It had been late all this time. I was really hoping it would stay gone for a few more days. I popped a few pills and kept it pushing. As the day went on the pains kept getting worse but I refused to let this pain get the best of me. I kept going. I cleaned up and awaited his arrival. Set everything up the way I wanted it in preparation for my evening plans. All while praying that these pains decreased. I started stumbling around. Lord help me. These pains are whooping me.

I had a talk with self... Come on Arketa keep going. Get it together girl... PUSH... Once again I shook it off and kept moving. My date arrived. I was so excited and everything looks like it's coming together. Dinner, conversation... everything other than this horrible pain that has become way bigger than my normal cramps. My evening is going perfect. I'm still trying to ignore it but he knows something is wrong with me. I'm trying not to tell him because though he always tries to make me his focus I have an announcement to make and I want that to be our focus right now.

Even though its Mother's Day, I want him to let me focus on pleasing him today because he tries to please me almost every other day. But because he sees me moving and adjusting, he doesn't let it go. So, I tell him I'm having really bad cramps. Well as the night progresses one thing led to another and we came up with the bright idea that sex would ease the pain.

I went to take a bath and he joined me. We both quickly jumped out of the water. No faster than we could get started, blood filled the tub. He jumps out, dresses, and leaves the bathroom. I jumped up but I couldn't really move because I didn't want to mess up the entire bathroom. In seconds the pains magnified, and it felt like someone was clawing my insides apart. I'm shaking, and I want to scream but can't. Tears fall. I'm trying to hold my breath because breathing makes it worse. It hurt so bad. It looks like someone turned on a water faucet and blood is rushing everywhere. I'm shaking and trying to clean it up at the same time.

What in the world is wrong with me? I cut the shower water on hot and try to stand there as long as I could. Hoping the fall of the hot water will help but it feels like my legs are about to give out from up under me. I feel weird like I need to push something out. I feel something sitting there and it hurts. But when I start to push it hurts even more. What am I supposed to do? I don't know where he went but I don't want anyone to see this. I'm embarrassed and bloody hand prints are all over the walls and the side of the tub. This is not how my night was supposed to go. I yell out in pain and I pushed thinking I was just trying to pass a clot.

Gross I know... but what I passed was so much more. It was a large piece of flesh in a ball. I didn't... I couldn't have... God say it ain't so... Is that... it couldn't be... My mind is all over the place. Is this what I think it is? The pains are calming down now. I get down on my hands and knees and pick up the ball. It is.... My announcement.... My baby.... I just pushed out my baby..... I sit it back down. I'm still bleeding heavy but I clean myself up and put some clothes on.

I go back into the bathroom and begin wiping the walls of my smeared, bloody hand prints. He finally walks back in to check on me. I look weak and not so good. I move the shower curtain and asked him to go get me a plastic bag. As I'm picking it up again he says "what the Hell?" Tears began to slowly move down my face. I put it in a bag and sealed it. I left the bag sitting on the counter and walked to the living room to sit down. I can't explain where I was in that moment but what I felt was devastation. He said
"You need to go to the hospital and get checked out"
"No, I'm alright. I just want to lay down for a little while then I'll think about going. I'll go. I just need time"

He looked disturbed. In my mind I was just trying to wrap my head around what just happened and what was sitting on my bathroom counter. I think he thought I didn't care but I was numb, hurt, and lost. I was so confused. I couldn't figure out how or why this would happen. He left. It was well into the wee hours of the morning. Eventually I got up and talked to a friend who had been through several miscarriages before. I was still in shock but she helped me keep it all together and got me to the hospital. They looked at the bag and examined me. I lost our baby and they cleaned me out.

The doctor stared at me and said my body aborted the fetus by bleeding it out. From that happening they discovered some other problems I had going on in my body. He said it was a blessing because they never would've noticed the other issues anytime soon. I guess it was a blessing and a curse but I still couldn't believe it. I met up with him a few days later and told him what happened. We argued and he began distancing himself from me. My relationship was never the same after that. It ended a few months later. I was upset and angry at how it happened but I wasn't all that surprised that it did.

I lost my baby on Mother's Day.... What a gift.... The worse gift I could've ever been given in life. It hurt like hell and that was the first moment I started to feel inadequate as a woman. I felt less than and even telling him was hard. It took a long time for me to shed another tear or show any emotions. It felt like a part of me grew cold that day. I felt numb inside. I was angry and I stuffed every feeling, every emotion and every heart ache deep down inside. I tried to live as if that moment never happened....

An Empty Life

Many days I hoped, wished, and prayed
For the continuous rain storm of sadness to go away
Desired for the raspy hands of death to rescue me
from the grasp of sorrows remains
I wanted to die
Tired of the false smiles and limited conversations
I speak when it's convenient cause under any
other circumstances there's hesitation
See actions speak louder than words
So often my eyes have seen more than my ears have heard
And in one breath I've swallowed more tears than the
clouds cry rain drops
My life has descended into a black hole of despair that
never stops
And I wanted to die
I've blinked into essence a reality that doesn't exist
Composed my dreams into fictions fabelized list
And often times fuel my life to die with words your
actions left behind
But the veil before your eyes has you too blind to see
That my truths aren't false excuses of explanation...
it's just me
Blocking out the thoughts of death
And in a state of pure exhaustion my trying has grown weary
I forcefully move through existence dreary
and in the midst of drought but my heart knows love
But can't help its doubts and with passing moments I
struggle to keep myself
From wanting to die
But I'm tired and speaking,
most times, it's more pointless than fulfilling
Cause in the end most still remain too blind to
understand me

See looks can be deceiving; nothing is all it's
cracked up to be,
And telling my story isn't always easy
When hidden inside I really
Want to die
But God Won't let me
And in the midst of my storm
My patience will send out my greatest blessing
The outcome will be my testimony
So death will have to keep on waiting
Until God has finished using me
Because under no circumstances
AM I ALLOWED TO DIE.

"Suicide"

Be prayerful. If you give the devil an entry way to get in, he is going to bust all the way through and try to take over. What do I mean by that? Well there are times when the devil will get into your mind and literally build a playground. When you think about a playground what do you see? Monkey bars... (You're just hanging around. You moving but you're not really going anywhere), a swing... (You're going back and forth but you stuck in one place. The only thing that keeps getting higher and higher is your emotions), a slide... (You start out feeling like you're on top of things and then all of a sudden you're spiraling down till you hit the bottom), a sea saw... (You're on an emotional roller coaster that you can't get off of.

One minute you're happy, the next minute you're sad. One minute you're up, the next minute you're down and nothing you do can change that). When the devil was given an entry way in my life, he jumped in and built a playground in my mind and started running amuck. I was so hurt and devastated and on such an emotional roller coaster that I couldn't get off of to the point that my friend and I wrote a book. It was called *101 Ways to Commit Suicide* but, nobody knew about it but us. Our desire to die was so real. People are too quick to judge a book by its cover without ever looking at the pages inside. People thought I had it all together. That I looked as if my world was completely full of happiness, rainbows, and glitter sprinkled on top. But, I was living an entirely different reality.

Every breath I took I wanted it to be my last. This hurt I had consumed me. I've never cried so much. I felt like nobody cared about me nor did they care about my feelings. Instead, they wanted to tell me how I felt instead of hearing how I was actually feeling. I was tired. I hated living with a passion. I tried church, I tried God and all I got was more heartache than I had before I walked in the doors. I keep praying. I'm screaming out to heaven asking God to help me but, things are only getting worse. I trusted them because they said I could. They said it was ok. They lied. They used my words against me. They twisted around what I said.

Why can't I die? Nobody will miss me if I'm gone. I feel empty, lost and lonely. But since prayer is what I know, praying is all I could do. Even in the midst of my foolishness I guess God must've been hearing me after all. When we wrote the book it was based off of stuff we had tried but didn't work. No matter what we tried to do it wouldn't work.

    I ended up destroying it because I didn't want to be responsible for anyone else's actions. I didn't want to feel guilty or responsible if someone else succeeded at the things I failed at. I didn't want that kind of accountability. I'm not quite sure what changed my mindset... I guess it must've been all the prayers going up and failed attempts. But every day that I cried over the situations I couldn't change or over another thing somebody said or did to me, the more I realized that in that moment my faith was based on the people that were coming or going out of my life. When you're in your element you act according to your element. So when I prayed it was because that was what I was told to do. Eventually, I transitioned into doing it because I knew that prayer would one day completely save and change my life.

Live Today

I decided to live again today
As hard as it may be
I decided to live again today
Though the problems kept coming
One right after another
never missing a blow or a beat
Whooping me....
So much is happening
I can't breathe
I'm looking for an escape from this reality
Life is hurting
Sending me downward in a spiral rapidly
Nothing to stop me
I'm losing my mind & I just need to be free
It's all set up the liquor, the pills, the rope,
the chair, & me
I think I'm ready...
1.... 2.... 3....
The decision wasn't easy
In that moment my circumstances
exceeded the faith in me
My chest is heavy
Breathes short & choppy
God, I know you said that you'll never
put more on me than I can bare
But this right here is too heavy a burden for me to carry
In that moment I knew somebody somewhere
besides me was praying
If I died today what kind of example am I setting for
those that were to follow me
When life gets too hard simply quit trying
NO... KEEP FIGHTING
In a drunken haze I leaped for what
I thought was a new destiny

But death too rejected me
Because in that moment
I decided to live again today

"LIVE"

A new me! It's time to create a new me. I'm too old to play the same games. It's the same game, but it's changing faces. I will pass. I am more than a conqueror. I can do all things through Christ who strengthens me. Life and death is in the power of the tongue and this is what I speak - life. Cover me Lord with your blood. I'm not what I should be, but I'm not what I used to be. Change me LORD. I can't do it on my own.

Dear God,

Put a burning desire down on the inside of me that I may worship and serve you. Light my soul on fire and keep me Lord. When my mouth can't speak, talk to me. Break my attitude that I may humble myself and bow to you. I hear their cries Lord, I see their pleas. Set fire to the desire on the inside of me. Let the blazes roar and rupture down on the inside. Hold me, love me, protect me. I can't do it on my own. Can't nobody... nobody do me like you, touch me like you. Can't nobody hold me like you, heal me like you... have your way Jesus! Stir up in me what you would have instilled in me. The bondage that holds my heart captive, remove it. Those things that are pressed down and covered up..... The hurt, the pain, the confusion, the doubt, be my comfort in an undetected storm. Be my peace in a river of misunderstandings, be my guide when I can no longer see, be my words when I can't speak, show up when I can no longer feel your presence. Have your way. Jesus, I'm calling your name. When nothing else can be said, Lord I'm calling your name Jesus. Jesus you said that no weapon formed against me shall be able to prosper, but I'm the weapon Lord. I'm the blockage, I'm standing in the way, and I'm standing in the need of prayer. Satan can't see what I write, but he hears every word I speak so this is my silent plea Lord. I can't do it on my own. It won't work. Jesus you're the only one who can help me when I can't help myself. You're the one I can call on in the midnight hour. You're the one who's never left me or forsaken me. You're the one who held me tight when I baptized my pillow in midnight tears, you're the one. You're the one who... Yes, Father you're the one. You were my sight when I couldn't see; You welcomed me when everyone else turned away. You eased the pain that others caused. You protected me when I was in harm's way. I don't understand everything that takes place God but do it in me Lord. You pulled me left when I wanted to go right. You kept me going straight when I wanted to take a detour. Thank You God. Take over me so that I don't stray away. Cover me Lord in Your Anointing. Anoint me in Your presence. Have Your way in me. I can't make it on my own. I'm coming out, I'm coming out dear God... You hear me I'm coming out, and I'm coming out better that I was when I went in. In Jesus' name I believe, but Lord help my unbelief.....

Amen

Better Than This

Today my mind had a fight with my heart
And though logic & reasoning spewed out
valid points from the start
My heart just wasn't trying to hear it
I placed others above myself who didn't deserve it
You would've thought I learned my lesson
but I kept doing it
Stupid......
Being used and abused I knew it
but I tolerated it
Didn't love it
But became content in it
Accepted it because I thought my love
would supersede it
But it didn't....
I put my needs on the back burner
to be an aid for those that ain't cared
nothing about it
But pretended to love me back to keep getting it
Lost sight of my self-worth and allowed it to
dwindle away with the dignity
That had just found me
Screamed many days to come to my senses
But instead I justified the actions that were
betrayed by reasoning
See the logic behind it was missing....
So though my mind could see what was happening
My heart stayed in the lead until it became my reality
Where I could no longer see what was happening
See I've dealt with more than my fair share of Bull S**t
Since the beginning of this relationship
But now all I seem to do is compromise
the essence of my self-worth to maintain it
So TODAY I had a fight with SELF.......

"360 Days"

On the average day if it begins good, it doesn't remain that way all day. Today was quite interesting on every level. I've begun to question myself as a result. Not in a bad way but just enough to see if I can understand clearly exactly what's going on. There're two things I desperately need right now... A.) A real job that I enjoy and B.) my own apartment. So during the times when I feel like the weight of the world rests solely on my shoulders, and I'm slow walking my way through the feelings of being inadequate and unable to measure up enough to make anyone happy, I can always have a sanctuary of solitude that is all my own.

A place that I can retreat to and not have to look at the unspoken words of disappointment written in yet another pair of loving eyes. But how can you peacefully get along with yourself? I've often wondered if the love that runs is a pity love. For that reason alone... is that what all the fuss is about? Or is it because I keep nagging you about what I see imperfect in you and you nag at me about the imperfections you see in me? Are we in turn attempting to fix what we don't like about ourselves in hopes to be better? Exactly who is the essence of me that you are in love with outside of the image that reflects you? Does the average love feel like this? Are my happy days actually happy if I cry at least once because of something said? Will the fussing between us grow to be such a nuisance that you become weary and walk away or will my silence draw a wedge between us that forces you to leave? Why am I something to be desired?

Is there a decision that can be made with no remorse when spoken out loud? There will never be enough words to explain the tear in my heart. I miss the smile I used to get when we enjoyed being around each other. I feel like the longer I'm with you the more my heart can no longer find contentment in the silence of sadness. Not only can't I tell up from down but I can't see us anymore. I can't feel us anymore. I've given all that I had and then some and it was never enough. I was never good enough? I was never enough. You need more. I just wanted to be enough. How can my heart survive like this? In one year I loved, lost, regretted, and recovered or at least began recovery to walk into this year starting life all over.

People came into my life that I am glad are gone. My trust.... Depleted, relationships... decapitated, me.... alone picking up the pieces. I finally understood the saying true friends are hard to come by. Evaluating everyone who calls me their friend and everyone I called mine... none of us really understood exactly what that term meant, but we all had our own interpretation. A true friend isn't with you because of what they can obtain from you. A true friend is gonna have your back regardless. There is no mistake or bad decision you can make in your life that could make them walk away from you.

Their love is unconditional. That's what I was looking for in my relationship. A friend and a companion. It took a while but I eventually started to realize that the relationship was one sided. One of the hardest things to discover is that the person you're in love with is using you. Wake up calls are sometimes the most difficult calls to receive. It seems like my bad days outweigh my good days but I know things can only get brighter from here.

Mirror Me

I'm trying to do right but wrong won't let me
I'm trying to do right but wrong won't let me
God I'm trying to do right but wrong won't let me
I'm trying to believe but the lack of trust only
allows me to believe as far as I can see
Life has always been my struggle and death
keeps rejecting me
I know that I'm strong but there's more pain than
love in my heart
And often times it's what breaks me before I even start
I know that I'm loved but there's parts of me that's
missing still searching
So most days I cry with the drips of my showers rain
caressing the aches from my wounds pains
Praying for the day when I find my stolen baby;
and just maybe
Find why life kidnapped her innocence, fractured her soul, and
buried her essence
With artificial pictures and broken promises
Portrayed one image but fed her the opposite
So forgive me but I can't believe this distorted visual
I've been given
In my most sacred chamber I know she's still living
Because my heart hasn't ceased from beating
I can still hear the echoes of her faint breaths breathing
and I can't be complete with her missing
I can hear the whispers of the meaningless
conversations lingering
the day when she was ripped from me
snatched from existence as if she never meant anything
The pressures of people's brutal fantasies
acted out embedded itself in me
Mounted roots from the planted seeds of its memory
And when the fists, rumors and humiliation

ripped my voice from me
as long as I was thinking I never forgot her ever existing
and it was then that my pen first took over remembering
so no matter how many successes I continued achieving
I'm not truly successful until we are reuniting
Because she's the peace that dwelled on the inside of me;
the foundation of my dreams
The balance between weakness and insecurity
The connection between my future and reality
She's the love songs Solomon chose to sing
The inner strength that told Job to keep believing
The secret voice that pushed Moses to keep leading
The light to my dark path when life's storms
shield my eyes from seeing
She's loves motivation…the stolen pieces of me my
heart keeps seeking
The reflection that stared back at me in the morning
The mirroring image of my security
Me still growing
I need to fill the void where she's missing
Every time I look in the mirror
I can only see what used to be
The moral of my story… I'm incomplete
Without the she in me torn away with history;
I'm nothing
And there's no freedom in me
as long as my heart is searching for what's missing
I need my inner me, my baby, the lost side of integrity
I NEED TO FIND ME.

"Big Dreams Then None"

Up until I was 11, I wanted to be a lawyer and a singer. By 13, I wanted to be a singer and a writer. At 16, I stopped singing all together but I still kept writing. I stopped singing because there was no longer any joy in it for me. It seemed like every time I opened my mouth to sing I was criticized, or I had to compete with someone and I didn't see the purpose in competing. I never did anything to make it a competition. I did it because I loved what I was doing. If I had to compete to do something, then I wasn't going to do it. The last time I sang it became a competition between me and another girl in the choir.

The choir director was in favor of the other person. They both talked mad noise which was so unnecessary. It's funny how at church people can make a big deal over such little things. To completely degrade a person just to be the one to get in front of a crowd of people and pretend for those few minutes that they are somebody great. They called me everything but the name I was given at birth. They tag teamed and clowned me so bad and the choir director was throwing us into each other like we were about to fight. I'm not... I won't do it... I had to take a step back.

Their words cut deep but I refused to shed a tear in front of them. The choir director's last words to me were "what on earth gives you the right to think you're better than her? Nothing about you is appealing. She got something and you're a nobody. What gives you the right to think you're great and worthy enough to be in front of a crowd? You're not even cute. You'll never be anybody". My reply was "I'm not trying to be better than anyone I'm just equal I..." Instead I just stopped talking mid-sentence. It wasn't worth it. None of this was worth it.

My life outside these doors was hell. I refused to come here and live in it too. If this is what I had to go through and hear in order to sing I could've just stayed at home. I get told how dumb and ignorant I am there all day long. This was supposed to give me a break. So I stood up, grabbed my stuff and walked out. I didn't go back to the choir. That one or any other one as a matter of fact. I didn't sing again from that day forward. I kept writing though because it was my voice when I didn't have one. My pages held my secrets. They contained the words that were beaten out of me yet on paper spoke volumes that could never be shared out loud with anyone.

My true identity was written in their pages and if ever read would paint picture after picture of every heartache, trial, joy, tribulation, emotion, and thought. I continued to write because there was something in it. There was something there. My writings gave me life in dead places and helped me find my way in the process. My pages allowed me to see everything in me I didn't like, absolutely couldn't stand, and the parts I wanted to know better. They kept me sane when I felt like I was losing my mind. Writing gave me comfort and understanding when life and people beat me down. It kept me breathing when I wanted that next breath to be my last.

My journals have been my mirror helping me find more than just my reflection. I was on a mission to find me. I kept writing so that I could live. I dreamed of being an internationally known poet and author. I wanted to be great. Yet, as always life happened and life was holding no punches and neither were the people. So, right around age 25 I stopped dreaming again. The older I got the harder it seemed to dream. To imagine that there is something or that I could have something bigger. That I was capable of achieving something more than what I have right now. I allowed people and circumstances to steal my dreams from me and not dreaming became easy as I just existed in life.

I Trusted You

I can never forget the day
you held me in your arms
and calmed my fears
When you gently wiped away
each and every one of my tears
And I Trusted You...
I can never forget how I felt
when you said you loved me
And that our future would make up
for what the past could never be
And I Trusted You...
Now I sit through depth of my sorrow
Wondering about Tomorrow
With my tears running like waterfalls
Streaming quickly from my eyes
At the thought that...
I Trusted You

"Just Trust Me"

Just trust me is the most honest lie I ever heard. People tell you to trust them. Believe in them. They're not gonna hurt you. They'll never betray you. But actions speak louder than words and more often than not my eyes have seen more than my ears have heard. I know some people mean well but they're not true to their word and most of them walk away. What does that say about me as a person if not one person is consistent? Maybe I need to find out what about me needs to change to keep people around. Or maybe I'm just too broken for people to stay or to make people be true to their word.

Dear God,

Tonight I'm going to do something I haven't done in a long time and that's talk to You. I don't want anyone else right now. I don't want to be around anyone else. I don't like where I am right now and I'm not doing anything to change that. I feel so far gone from You that I don't know how to get back. I feel as though I don't have anyone in my corner anymore. And every time I pick up a drink or smoke to attempt to get a moments peace I become even more depressed. I'm not happy and I haven't been for a long time. My soul hurts so bad I can feel its pains in every heart beat. I think of how things used to be when I felt loved and was able to give it back. When I thought my life changed for the better and it ended up worse. I keep picturing the night I poured my heart out to her and she prayed over me and we cried together. Now I'm alone because though we made it through that moment it was too much for her to bare so now I'm back alone. When I was once mentored and prospering & now I'm heading straight to hell. I hate the way things are but I don't feel like I can do it by myself and I have no one with me. I'm sorry I strayed so far away. Please find me. Everything I fought not to become I have and I'm miserable. I want somebody to hold me in their arms and let me know I'm loved.

Let me know they're there. I believed my bond with her was so strong for me because she gave me everything I dreamed of and more emotionally. Also everything I desired spiritually but it was all taken from me. The pattern got started. I was reeled in and then it was discontinued. Why am I still here? Why? I feel like I wake up every morning dead and I go to sleep every night dead. I no longer have an in between. God, Father, Jesus can You just wrap your arms around me and hold me close and don't let go. Squeeze me tight. I need a true hug and some true love... not just another temporary fix. God can You let me know You're here holding me? I need some attention. Please hear my cry Lord in Jesus name....

Amen

Confused

No matter how hard I try not to be hypocrite
I've discovered often times
I am a Compromising Christian
God stays away at least an arm length
anything closer I might lose it
Most nights I dreamed of the salt of my tears
cleansing away the dirt of my daily sins
Prayed to Our Father
while looking for love in the form of rainbow kisses
And though it wasn't right I did it
Not because I wanted to but because
it was the only place I was continuously
Wanted, accepted, and hearing it, "I Love You"
Still in church I had the best of two worlds
ministering into the lives of
others but rightly wasn't living it
God said, "Choose this day who ye shall serve"
but I didn't
I was no different than the ones who preached
gospel but never seen it
Strangled life from the flocks they lead
Quoting John 3:16 and calling it Revelation 4:23
CONFUSED

My soul had too many fractures that needed healing
But I stayed hidden behind a wall of
misery although welcomed,
God couldn't reach me
I was a shape shifting chameleon constantly
changing but never fully converting
Most of the time I had nothing
but was above poverty
Believing I was rich according to my Father in glory
A ½ of a step away from being homeless

and just got disconnected by We Energies
But I'm blessed
My bills are past due and
I'm still helping everybody else
Cause what I got isn't enough to cover me
so by giving to you
maybe something can find one if not both of us
I didn't give 10% so I had to make up the difference
helping others was a must
I felt as though my good deeds would make up
for the separation between God and me
And though often times my faith was weak
and I failed to believe
God still loved me
It was there all along but I was too busy searching to receive
CONFUSED

But God said "A double minded man is unstable"
I couldn't get in where I fit in
so instead I got in where I was able
Which is why I was always confused
There's no way you can serve
God doing whatever you want to
You've got to choose
God didn't weigh out his options
when he created you
Your prayers may not have been answered
when you wanted but He always came through
No matter how many times you fell down
He repeatedly forgave you
You've got to decide on whose
battlefield you'll get used too
But you've got to be the one to choose
Him after all He already chose you.

"Confused"

In life I wanted two things. I wanted to be beautiful and I wanted to be loved. I never felt like I was either, so I continuously sought after them both. Love more so than beauty because I felt like since I had cute moments I didn't have to chase beauty as hard. I never would have imagined being wrapped up like this. Giving my heart away so easily, mistrusting and painfully hurting as a result but I went where the love was. I followed it until the reality of the situation slapped me and every since, solitude has been my closet companion. For years now the search for love and solitudes silence has been my best friends, especially when I had everything stripped away from me. Stolen, as I stood by externally watching and wondering why.

Imitating, yet wondering where the faith in all of this is. What do you do when The Word in you becomes weary? What do I do when The Word becomes so jumbled while reading it that I'm unable to comprehend? When the lyrics of my prayers begin to continuously trample over each other so severely that I could no longer speak? And what about when I write? Writing has been the longest lasting love in my life and now I have to write in code so no one else can understand. You know those unwanted eyes that scan through these pages looking for something to make an issue out of. The understanding is so messed up the questions on my brain are tearing me apart. So, all I can do is write and even then my thoughts are scrambled.

Reality slapped me in the face today as I realized the main reason I am not willing to let go of a lot of things. It's because I'm in a comfortable and familiar place right now. Yeah some days are harder than others, but I fear that if anything changes I'll be left totally alone again. Left struggling and fending for myself and struggling harder than I was before the comfort. I haven't yet convinced myself that much of this battle is worth fighting for and if I don't believe it within myself I won't make it through the process. After having a life of inconsistency, believing in yourself or your own ability isn't something that comes second nature to you. If no one has ever really believed in you or helped you find your way in life, you spend a lot of time just wandering around in life trying to find your way. It's hard to believe in yourself when you never learned how to believe in the truth about anything because everybody around you told so many lies. Therefore, I've always acted as my worst enemy. I subject myself to stuff I shouldn't. I treat myself like a third-class citizen in life and I treated God the same way I treated myself. I think when you are trying to learn to believe in yourself and your own ability, the best way to do that is to have someone in your corner who loves you unconditionally. Someone who believes in you and your ability to accomplish things and conquer the world enough for the both of you until you learn how to do it for yourself. That's what I did. I hung onto them believing in me and my ability.

The reason I make so many mistakes is because for so long I have been in the church but the church ain't been in me. Making decisions and not understanding the consequences but one day everything's going to change and things are going to be different. I have dreams of a totally different person. Not who I see today. I'm beginning to accept that I'm not what I used to be and I'm grateful. But I'm not where I should be and that's what keeps playing in my mind. I think about everyone who's ever come in and out of my life. I realized I've spent so long living my life fitting other people's fantasies that I lost sight of who I was. So in the meantime, I began to have an "I don't care attitude".

It felt like my heart was getting numb and I was becoming cold hearted and mean. I developed such a hatred for so many people. I just couldn't look at people the same anymore. I've tried to approach things from the Christian perspective and it got to the point where I couldn't even pray no more. The ones I thought were supposed to have my back let me go, talked about me, betrayed me, and I was devastated. I hold a hurt deeply rooted down on the inside of me that won't go away. I can't cry out my frustration, scream out my miseries and pains, yell out my anger, nor smoke out and drink my problems away. I'm resting on the dark side, so far gone from the light I can't find my way home. I have no joy and peace. I need someone in my corner. I need help. I need someone to pull me out of what I'm in and no one's there.

I'm all alone. My relationship with God has to get better though. I believe, but too often I doubt myself. I've done so much wrong that I feel incapable of actually doing right. I'm actually scared much of the time that I'll fail. My prayer life is somewhat lazy and I always say tomorrow I'll do better, but then tomorrow comes and nothing's accomplished. If I don't hurry up and begin spending more time with God I'll lose everything including my life.

So I'd better get it together, but I can't feel it in my heart and that's what makes it hard. I keep telling myself faith ain't built upon feelings. It's built upon beliefs. So though I believe, God help my unbelief because the first thing the devil does to get you off course is to get you upset. Can't nobody build you like you can. Nobody knows what you've been going through like you do and you can't just talk about getting up. You've got to GET UP. If you follow through you'll realize the Father missed you just as much as you missed Him... even more. He's waiting on you. God is ready for you to be stable for Him. If you don't like who you are, then change. Satan will play on how you feel. You ain't got to prove nothing to the devil. Know who you are.

Whispering Dreams

Beside still waters I dream
Of one day becoming something new
Listening to natures call
In my dreams I see you

Watching the sun reflect off the water
As it shines down through the trees
I reminisce about the times we had
Then I fall down on my knees

While on my knees I call on the Lord
As I cry out tears of pain
Wishing you were still here with me
Hurting that things are no longer the same

Wondering what my place in life is
Wondering what still remains
Awakening hearing soft voices
Gently whispering out your name.

"Gone for Real"

I thought it was a dream when I saw you staring at me with your mouth opened wide. I dropped my board game and ran to you. Shaking you... calling you "mama...mama..." You didn't respond to me. I ran to get help but they said it was too late. I thought it was a dream so I didn't cry for you. When you were sick I prayed for you to get better. I prayed for the pain you were in to stop. I guess I should've prayed for God to leave you here with me when He changed your situation. I waited for a long time to wake up from this dream. It was a nightmare I couldn't believe was happening and I couldn't stop it. I couldn't change the ending no matter how hard I tried. Maybe I should've had a different request. I needed you. You were my best friend. I have so many questions I need answers to.

Who's going to answer them for me? Everything is my fault now and I'm alone in this. Why did you leave me? Why didn't you take me with you? Ask God why didn't He do a two for one special? I want to go. I want to be with you. I'm trying everything I can think of but I'm still here. Ask God if He's punishing me? Ask God what did I do to deserve this? You were the only somebody that really loved me and now you're gone. Who's gonna talk to me about life and life stuff? Who will I ask all my questions to? So much is happening around me. Everything around me has changed and one day I stopped being scared and I started welcoming it.

Did you stop loving me? Were you mad at me? Is that why you left? Mama, I still loved you. Every day I dreamed of you coming back to me. I sit in the window waiting for you to come back to me. I looked for you to come walking down the street but you don't. So instead I walk down the street hoping you'd come walking around the corner but you never show up. I want to run into your arms again but you never show. So instead I lay where you laid. I need you to show up. I can't do this by myself. I need you to lay in my bed with me one more time and just talk to me. I miss our talks. I need us to go book shopping again. Reading just isn't the same now. Come back to me please. Am I the cause of this? Why did you go? You couldn't fight anymore? Couldn't you hang in there a little while longer? Come back to me.... PLEASE.... I went to school today and watched the moms drop their kids off and kiss them goodbye. We had a party and parents brought treats. I looked for you to come but you never showed up. You said you'd always be there for me but you're missing everything. Why won't you show up? You're never coming back to me are you? I guess not because I started growing up today and I looked for you but you never showed up.

You Are Not Alone

Baby believe me when I tell you that
For every trial you've faced
There's someone else that's seen it too including me
See sleep don't always come easy
I can recount many times when I'd close my eyes and
fall lost in miseries companionship
Until my own reflection grew too blind to even see me
So I learned at an early age to build a bridge over my pain
With all that life hasn't taken away
Yearned for the love that captivated my artificial self-worth
And brought safety to my darker days
Mirrored silhouetted shadows of inspirations
that dwindled with dignity
that never found me
Because my life has always consisted of dirty finger tips
and saturated lips of freshly slaughtered innocence
Shaking fast on dirty store tops and molded floors
As I walked suicidal highways across manifestations and
manipulated secrets locked behind closed doors
Past burned bridges that captured the remains of my soul
So believe me when I tell you that you are not alone

I've swallowed so many depressions that despair
began to look like a sanctuary of peace
I've seen black rainbows stain cloudy days while drowning in the
essence of your own emotions begging for the pains to cease
As life took pleasure in degrading and humiliating me as it
proceeded to give me it's all
But I still held on and I still stayed strong because I had to
For as I grew my heartaches they multiplied by two
And when I reached capacity's limit I still went through
Until I began to cry yesterday's tears on today's journey
Alone, because love was never a word in my vocabulary

See for me this here hasn't even marked the beginning
I battled deceits that lurked in the dark
Clutched dawn's side as death stood over my shoulder
and my role as an actress would start,
LIFE was my stage
Whoever I had to be to survive is what I portrayed
And I could confirm and transform into anything
I'd be the greatest superstar this world has ever seen
But if I could triumph over my obstacles
then so could you
And if need be I'll walk some of them same roads
over and over and over again
Just so you won't be alone
to prove to you that you aren't on your own
And to let you know that baby it's not just you
The same trials that trip you up today,
many of us have hurdled too
So you are never alone.

"You Can Run but You Can't Hide"

When someone does something to violate you that's a really hard thing to come back from... To live through. Your life isn't the same anymore. You see the world through an entirely different set of lenses. You trust no one... not even yourself. At least I didn't. I pretended to be ok. I pretended to still be the same. Some of them told me they were sorry. They didn't mean it and I wanted to believe them. I needed to believe them because how could love hurt like this. Why would love betray me? What did I ever do to it but chase after it? I blamed myself because I trusted the wrong people. I believed in them so anything that happened to me as a result was my fault. I feel like the best parts of me were destroyed beyond repair.

Who was going to be in my corner if everyone in my corner was betraying me? At one point I even woke up out of my sleep to someone threatening me and telling me I sleep too hard. This was because they'd been standing there watching me for a minute and no one can help you. What kind of help do you seek when there are pastors with police officers as best friends helping them get away with the things they do? I suffered the consequences of being disobedient, but my silence kept me alive. If I didn't know anything else I knew how to survive. Occasionally I still look in the mirror at my back where the knife cut me down the dip of my back as I tried to escape the corruptness. After that I retreated into doing what I was instructed until I could plan my next escape.

No, this wasn't a cult I was in. I just went to church and trusted the wrong people in leadership who wanted what they wanted no matter what I was wearing. No matter what I said. No matter what I did. There was no escaping it and they had no problem letting me know it. It was all about sex and power and after a while I just began to have sex just because it was what was wanted. Not that I actually wanted to do it but I felt like it was better to give it up than to have it taken from me again. So I lay on my back and let them do whatever it was they were going to do and waited for them to finish. There were many days I'd look in the mirror and despise what looked back at me. I shed tears but never really cried. I can't. I tried to hide from my past... from the things I went through. But at some point and probably when you don't want it to but things have a way of catching up with you.

Surviving is hard but it's doable. Especially when you can find someone... the right someone, a God sent someone to be there with you in the darkness. To help guide you out because no one can stay hidden forever and the process of coming out is really difficult but it's so worth it. The struggle, the fight, the release, the revelation, and the freedom... it's all worth it. The fight to freedom is hard but the reward of the freedom makes it all worth going through. The things you learn along the way you can cherish forever. Those are the most valuable triumphs on the journey because you're not only finding self but you're finding others who are broken just like you.

Others trying to fight their way out because they want to be free too. You realize you are not alone. In the midst of attempting to swing back at the blows I was getting hit with, my eyes opened. I saw that as a result of everything I endured, I become accustomed to catering to everyone else and neglecting myself but, I woke up in my fight. I realized today that I go hard for everybody else but I always leave myself lacking. I wonder why that is and why it took me so long to notice. But today when I realized it, it really pissed me off at myself. Because in realizing that, I also noticed that no matter what you do or how much time you invest in someone else's vision, it'll never be enough. Your efforts will be in vain. I stopped dreaming.

I stopped planning. I stopped investing in me and I gave up on me. That was my number one mistake. I didn't feel worthy enough to prosper but my worth was based off of the opinions of others. They said it to me so much that I started saying it to myself. My mind was strong enough. I used to dream of building a legacy so that my children will have something to be proud of. But, when I realized I'd never give birth to one that dream went with that reality and added to my unworthiness. Nevertheless, today lit something in me. It added a fuel to the fire that burned deep inside me and I began to dream again. Not only did I begin to dream but I began to create and invest in me and my future. I realized it's time to go harder for me than I've ever gone for anybody else. Today I felt like I could conquer the world by taking one bite at a time. But, I had to chew quickly because I've got a lot of years to make up for. Today marked the first day I began going hard for me because I deserved better.

Though I Believe

Though I believe God help my unbelief
I'm trying to do right but nothing about my road is easy
There's no master key or cute book of antidotes
wrapped all pretty, laced in pink
My temptations are great and my faith is weak
I'm trying to hold on but I'm losing my stability
Trust and patience ain't never been strong suits for me
And every day it's something...same, old, or new
I'm tired of being scared, looking over my shoulder, and praying
I'm always praying but my prayers don't seem
like they're getting through
And I know what you're capable of because
I've already seen you move
But my heart has reached capacity's limits,
I'm at wits end, and I don't know what to do
I'm trying hard to follow but I desire to break all the rules
I'm trying to be committed but I feel like I don't have a clue
I work hard daily to strengthen my weaknesses
and change my ways
Fall out of my routine and increase my faith
but it's not easy and no one said it would be
I do the best I can with what I have
and I've finally learned to love me
And though I believe God please,
please help my unbelief
Help me change the things in me that my
insecurities won't allow me to reach
Teach me to stop searching
for what I already have
Change the key to my future
so it's not living in the past
Give me the endurance to hang in there
and not give in to defeat
Train me to stay focused when

I feel like I'm too weak
Give me guidance and direction so
I don't stray into my own thing
Heal my heart from the aching
memories in which it clings
Renew my mind that I may be made whole
I've been incomplete for too long,
I'm reaching out,
I can't make it on my own
So though I still believe
God please help my unbelief
The areas in me that my insecurities
won't allow me to reach
I'm trying to do right
but nothing about my road is easy

THE FIGHT...

"On the Outside"

Sometimes it's hard to fight in the spirit when you spend so much time fighting in the physical and you're weak and wounded. When life has beaten you senseless and life seems like it's not even worth living and all people seem to do is tell you to pray. How do you encourage yourself when you barely know how? What strength do you hold on to when you have nothing left? How do you keep going when everybody around you is betraying you? When life has more downs than up but something inside you tells you to keep going. It'll get better. When does the better come and how much worse can it really get? I just want love and like everything else in my life since my mama died, it missed me. I think I died with her that day.

Everybody keeps talking about God but where is He. Does being a Christian mean a lifetime of misery because I have an abundance of it? I keep talking to God but is He really hearing me because I feel like I'm fighting alone. I'm lonely. Even when I go to church I'm lonely. I sit by quietly waiting on something to happen but I don't see anything. I need it to hurry up, to come fast, to be quick. If I'm getting whooped in the physical what makes you think I won't lose in the spiritual. I'm stronger in the physical than I am in the spiritual. Today I got hurt in ways I never would've imagined. Shattered to pieces, lost and wondering where to go from here but still having to find a way to keep fighting unless they destroy me first....

"On the Inside"

You've got to talk to the Lord. If you want something from God you've got to put something out there. Ask God to change your mind. Sometimes you've got to literally fight your way out. You've got to tell the devil I'm not staying like this. I can't stay this way no longer. You will not have your way. I'm fighting my way out of this situation. You can't live in God's will with one foot in and one foot out. We're fighting something... We're fighting the enemy, but in order to do battle with the devil you've got to come off his side and move. You've got to be violent in the spiritual realm to reach God. You've got to learn how to seek the face of the Lord. You've got to get to a point in your life when people don't impress you and God totally has control over you. Sometimes you need wisdom & revelation to get through the storm. In the midst of the storm you can't always see the answers to your questions. But, if you ask God to reveal it to you, He can reach you in the midst of the storm and show you.

Prayers have to come through the devil's territory but you've got to keep praying and God will send you other angels to help you get through the storm. The war is first natural then spiritual. We are in war. Look at all the young black men dying in the streets today. We can see it naturally but we've got to come against it spiritually. Sometimes you've got to take a stand against something bigger than you. Speak out against things bigger than you. If you don't tap into the revelation of God that helps you tap into who you are in the spirit realm, you'll leave out the same way you came in. Your mouth tells what your heart is thinking of. You keep asking when but God doesn't run on your time. He runs on His time.

God's strength is made perfect in weakness. The reason we're not seeing a mighty move of God is because you're sitting back waiting on God to send your blessings on remote control so you can sit back, push a button and get a miracle. But in order to get a miracle, you're going to have to be willing to be controversial, talked about, criticized, laughed at, and say like Job, "though he slay me, yet will I trust Him." In the midst of all the chaos, God will be in the midst doing His business. He can do business in the worst situations and not stop the situation taking place. He will still get the glory in the midst of it all. He could not deliver you from it but, deliver you while you're in it. He'll allow you to go through it and keep you from it all at the same time.

Watchful Words

Judge not less ye be judged
The words you speak today
Could lead to the drenching of the souls
tomorrow unplugs
As peace gathers on mountain tops
and reign down melodies
That embraces the hurting heart your
tongue left to bleed
Until sanity caresses your soul with a
divine since of need
Surpassing all the understanding that
blinds your sight
And though you trust are still forced to
walk through the valley of the
shadows of death
Like a dog waddling in his own vomit
Continuously going back
to the same old mess
Looking for a quick remedy when the
simplest honest answer
Is written and made plain for all to
see....

"Going Back"

Despite how much love we give and receive there are many people that don't want you to love. People that claim to love you but in reality want to destroy you. They set out to shatter the essence of who you are because they can see what you have the potential to become. I look at my life and my journey for love and in my mind I thought people loved me. But, in my heart I couldn't feel it so when they did stuff to me that hurt me I just told myself they were loving me the best way they knew how. So, I spent years seeking out what I desired and advised others on but never really knew. I looked at all the lessons I've learned along my journey. Though some experiences I would love to do over, I wouldn't trade the lessons I learned from them because the lessons were full of priceless information.

They spoke volumes about life. For example, remember ye not the former things, neither consider the things of old. Behold, I will do a new thing. Going back to what God had delivered you out of is like a dog going back to and eating that vomit. Why go back to what held you captive once you've been set free? What kind of sense does that make? When you were bound you were begging to be free. So, now you have to do what you have to do to save your soul and make sure it stays free. With age comes wisdom. So to get free you've got to change your mindset. To change your mindset you need to change the way you think, the way you walk, the way you talk.

Face your situation and don't run. Don't give the devil a foothold in your life to destroy you and defeat you. You can read all day but it doesn't matter if you don't know how to apply it. Ask God what's next, cast down what's unlike God, put action behind your words. Faith is an action word. Sometimes you have to learn a scripture backwards and forwards so when the enemy attacks you, you can speak God's word and the enemy can flee from you.

Big Girl Blues

Being a big girl ain't always easy
I forced my body to reflect the image
I saw every time I looked at me
UGLY
And though it's beautiful to some
I could never see its beauty
See I became fat for a reason
Me
five feet, 110 with a banging body
From the pulpit to the streets
Everybody wanted a piece of me
But the attention wasn't always welcoming
So after countless people attempting
to get from me what I wasn't offering
I decided to change what they'd see
There's nothing worse than someone
standing in front of me yelling
"Shut up Bit*h I'll take ya sh*t"
and mean it
I couldn't believe it
"No" was no longer a word that contained meaning
This became the first of a handful to
take my innocence from me
With each jab it stabbed away another piece of me
Stole a youth that apparently
I was no longer worthy of having
So every day I eat away
the tears I never shed.....

"Big Girl Blues"

I am a foodie and I have a love affair with food. Although I have specific requirements for what I want I still want it in abundance. Yep, I'm fat for a reason. Hello, my name is Arketa and I'm an emotional eater. I eat food to help me swallow my emotions instead of expressing them. Why don't I express them? Because I don't know how or sometimes it just seems easier to eat them than to share them. But that's not the only reason. See... growing up, being emotional wasn't allowed in our house. I was taught to be stern and that's what I am. Showing signs of emotion meant you were weak and I was weak for far too long. That's also the reason why I'm fat now. Because I was weak.

When I was skinny I was easily over powered and each time someone over powered me they took another piece of me with them. Every blow in every beating I took... Every blow I took period was another piece of me dying. And the pieces I had left they took from me when they raped me, when they betrayed me, when they told me they were sorry. It was an accident and it would never happen again but it did. Food was something I could control. Nobody wanted the big girl. In most eyes she was ugly and so I allowed that to become me. I feel like the less desirable I made myself the less people will want me. The word NO meant nothing. It has no meaning when a person wants what they want and sometimes there's nothing you can do about it.

My fat rolls around with me daily like a security blanket but I don't know how secure it is because most days I still feel scared. I can't stand crowds. People make me nervous. It gets hard to breath. If I know I'm going to be in a crowd I have to mentally prepare myself and even then sometimes I still panic because I feel like I'm putting myself at risk for something to happen. I never got my power back when they took it from me and I never lived again either. I just simply ate. I eat my miseries, my sorrows, my rejects, my fears, my hesitations, and my tears. I eat my fat girl blues where the pounds make the playing field level.

Transparency

She called me with one request, to be transparent
And as hard as it sounded to me I agreed
Because despite the fear I felt everything in me screamed
I could trust her....
Trust... One thing I normally don't do
but because it's you asking I will today
So after the pleasantries the next few words
she spoke echoed in me daily
They act as a continuous reminder
of the agreement we made
She needed me to be transparent
Transparent: easily seen through, recognized, or detected: open, made visible...
Now in reality this has been the most
difficult thing ever asked of me
Because it required me to look at
myself in the mirror and speak honestly
It required me to look at the dark hidden spaces
that I cared not to see
Face open festered wounds taped
down with band aids that
I prayed would go away but stayed
Tucked in corners behind walls that
caused me not to see them
I had to look at me even though the hatred
for what stared back at me was my reality
Since I've always hidden inside me this
was by no means going to be easy
I no longer saw the need for talking
And in my quietness I've stuffed decades of feelings
that ruptured when being pushed beyond belief
This was hard for me
Emotions I never saw or felt coming
No amount of tissue could wipe away the

feelings I was experiencing
And though every day I wanted to quit
because the images that stared back at me
were too hard for me to see
I agreed to be transparent
So no matter the cost I had to bare it
In order to stay true to my word
I didn't see it then but I quickly learned
that she was helping me save me
I was self - destructing but since the world was my stage
I portrayed the image that everything was ok
but every time she saw me she looked straight through me
I don't know if it was my eyes or my soul
but something was snitching on me
And she just needed me to be transparent
Then she reached out for some assistance
To help me in my transition out of simple existence
and needed me to trust her when
she said everything would really be ok
This is the moment I had to step out on faith
Because she needed me to dig deep to pull up
the root of my misery
The deeply buried secrets that my grave would share with me
and trust her to handle it with care
So I did and I began to share
I placed my secrets before her and watched
as she listened to each situation revealing its lesson
And even when my past manifested in my reality,
fear started to consume me,
and I wasn't strong enough to stand on my own
She taught me to stand on the wings of others
until I could stand alone
and she stayed with me
She placed my burdens at
Gods throne and asked him for guidance
as she helped me transition and in the midst
All she needed was for me to continue to be transparent

"Streams of Consciousness"
(Moment of truth with self)

    I had a dream last night that I was somebody important and I was to someone else what I allowed her to be to me..... It's hard for me to tell her the truth but I keep doing it. Even the lies I tell myself to make things ok are truths eventually. I share with her all the craziness. I wonder if it's ever too much. The things that if she wasn't on the other end of my phone to hear it for herself it would seem too unrealistic to be true. My family does the absolute most and I probably do too sometimes. But even though I share everything with her I just want to shield and protect her from everything and everybody including me... to keep her safe and pure from all this corruptness. On the flip side of things, even though she desires to know me in my entirety, I feel like I'm starting to grow silent out of fear that I'll be rejected once all sides of me are revealed.

    But I was told to be transparent and I agreed to it. Why did I agree to it? I didn't know any better. Was I foolish for agreeing? No, cause there is a benefit to it. How will I be in the end? Am I scared? I have my moments where I'm nervous, moments where I'm scared, & moments where I'm terrified but I don't say anything. But sometimes I think she just see's it even if I'm hiding it. Most of my life has been spent in fear, rejection, chaos, & pain. It all comes second nature to me like breathing. Right now I'm flooded with the memories of who I was and where I come from. The moments in time I haven't exposed her to yet. I'm trying to mentally be ok with showing her my insecurities, more wounds, the heartache I caused and still cause myself... I know this is the route I need to go in order to find the woman I desire to be but it's such an ugly road.

    So I'm searching for beautiful moments so that we can have beautiful conversations and not just the sad and ugly ones but, I can't find any. I want to show her that I have the potential to be really beautiful even in our conversations. I tried to tell God too. That I was beautiful... but then I tried to look in the mirror and tell myself and all I saw was the shame of where I came from and what I've come through. I tried to figure out how to be ok with all that and still be beautiful. I realized how much of my past is affecting my present. I'm trying to figure out how to move forward into my future without destroying it. Like what do I want out of life? Where do I want to go? Why do I feel like it's so bad to dream again? Everybody around me has dreams and goals. I encourage so many of them to achieve it but then I sit stuck trying to see what's going to happen. How can you build up nothing to make it better? Screaming right now! I can't believe I'm doing this. Ok girl keep going..... She'd tell you to keep going. What else are you thinking?

    I think I want to be able to look at me how they see me... how she sees me. It's interesting that her responses contradict everything I see in me. I see the ugliness that I try to dress up into something. I see the flaws that I try to convince myself make me flawless. I see the physical flaws that I try to keep hidden like the fattest parts of my body or the jacked up parts of my face. Which is why I prefer to have long hair that hangs on the sides of my face... It covers the ugly parts but right now I'm wearing this ponytail cause these braids wouldn't do what I needed them to. Now I'm ready to take them out and put in some weave that will. How can I tell a beautiful story in such an ugly place but I still keep looking for one?

    I've got to have one somewhere. How can you work with people and hear their stories all day long then sit up with me all night and listen to more ugliness? I've got to find a break in all the ugliness in order to keep it going. I've got to find the beautiful but where is it? Is my poetry beautiful? Not from what I read last night. It's just as distorted as I am. I guess because my work is a reflection of me. I don't think I'm ready for this release. Maybe I should push it out another year. Maybe I'll be in a better place then. Maybe I'm too dark for it right now. Do my words really matter? Do I really have something important to say? If I can't find my beauty big, I wonder what's the likelihood that I'll find it if I ever become 70 pounds lighter. I want to lose the weight but losing it terrifies me because I feel like I'm setting myself up to be a target again. What will I do if I lose all this weight and become a target again? What if I do all this work on me and it happens again? It'll destroy everything she's invested in me and I don't even know if I'll be able to tell her it happened again. I don't know if I could let her be there through that. Maybe I should just stay big. Nobody really likes the big girls....

I'm thinking about combining the chap book of poems in a Hidden Heart with my Journal Entries and turning it into something. Letting it be like the tell all. A lot of times when people come from the streets into the church you feel like you have to be perfect first. I think my journals and the realness of them, the prayers, the stories, and the lessons all show the raw imperfections of my process. But at the same time, it also reveals everything that I've kept hidden in my heart for decades. Had it not been for talking to her and her wanting to know every aspect of me, I might not have ever revealed anything that was hidden there because of the heavy amount of shame and embarrassment that came along with it. In mentally preparing to go deeper into these conversations with her I wonder how I'll be able to look at her again.

How will I be able to face her... Facing her... looking at her while exposed and ashamed. I'm putting too much thought into it. But she keeps telling me that she's there and I think she really got my back. It feels weird to know that against everything you've ever felt or even thought about yourself. I think because she genuinely loves me for real and cares about my well-being, part of me wants to protect her from the broken parts of me. The parts of me that aren't healed yet for fear that if I don't I might scratch, hurt, or wound her unintentionally. I want to keep her safe to make sure it lasts forever. From our relationship, friendship, & sisterhood though I also realized that in order to be around real love... true love... in order to have it, it requires you to be vulnerable. This is my first lesson in it which is why it's so hard to accept. It's weird to know that there's a possibility that the weight of who I was or who I am might not make her walk away.

As I begin to expose myself to her I'm realizing more and more about me. Areas of me I thought I would never see again. Areas of me I never wanted to face to begin with because I didn't like its appearance. I'm not sure if it's ok to get used to having her so close to me. I'm not even sure if it's ok because if I do get used to her being there and then she decides to leave me, like everyone did then I'll no longer have anyone to lean on. But if I just pull back and limit that connection and she decides to walk away, because the weight of who I am was too much to bare then I'll be hurt. But, I'll be ok because I didn't have all of me invested in the relationship. In dealing with her so up close and personal I realize it's kinda like dealing with God. Not that she is God or that I look at her as a god but, in the since that I treat God just like I treat myself. Like a 3rd class citizen and I view Him in the same manner that I view others. The same way I waiver in my relationship/sisterhood with her is the same way I waiver in my relationship with God. It's difficult for me to be completely open & vulnerable with Him.

    I find it hard for me to expose all aspects of me to Him. I struggle with completely letting myself go because I feel like I need to be guarded. In this process though I'm learning to trust beyond the althoughs... beyond the limitations... and beyond the walls I built to protect me. I think that as I am learning that, it's ok to be vulnerable because someone will still be there. Love requires vulnerability. It's ok to open up and to want better and to be better and to walk in who I should've been all along. But, that got distorted along the way. But if I reveal my truth...... If you can be with me in all my randomness & ratchetness.... I've always been a shape shifting chameleon. I've always conformed or transformed into something and this is the first time where there is nothing for me to transform or conform into. All I can be is me (LAWD smh) and that's a lot lol. If only you knew! I have to face 2, 10, 20, and 30 year old insecurities.

    My mind is all over the place smh. Who would've ever thought that love would be a risk when it's real? How can you love someone so genuinely and they've never done anything to deserve it? That was the first question I asked myself. It's funny how much she sees that I think I'm hiding and I feel like God sees me like that lol. He notices the little things and then sends me things or people to bring forth in me what He needs to come out. He does it in order for me to be ok with getting closer to God. I prayed and asked God to show me who I really am and help me. Show me how to walk into my grown woman. So He sent me another angel without wings that was able to begin to reveal the real me that is covered, hidden, and buried. He then began to use her to teach me how to be ok with the person that is. I'm learning how to express myself and be ok with putting that out there. It's funny how her love tries to chase my fears away. I'll be scared or nervous about something and she'll be like... "it's ok. You don't fully trust me yet but just watch and I'll show you". She never says just trust me. She always says I'll show you. That's remarkable to me because I've heard countless words in my lifetime that always amount to handfuls of empty promises. But, actions speak louder than any words that could ever be spoken. If I dream again it would be.....

Love Me

I wanted you to love me...
I needed you to love me...
I yearned for you loving me...
And as artificial as it may be
I was willing to hold on to it by any means necessary
As long as it pretended to fill the emptiness inside me
Looking for love in ALL the wrong places
Stained my sheets with secret faces
Even subjected myself to deadly situations
Just so you could love me
I converted my image to reflect unknown identities
Conformed my mind to sacrifice what
God placed on the inside of me
I aborted my soul for empty
I love you's with no meaning
I got trapped in scandals by
Just trust me's that played on my insecurities
But yet I craved for someone anyone to
Just love me
I even tried to use sex among many things
to build my self-esteem
But when I got up I felt even lower
than I did in the beginning
It didn't fill the void
at the end of the day I still felt empty
But I learned you can't sacrifice your dignity for 3 words
you've never seen or understood its meaning
But because I knew of its existence
I had a deep rooted desire for someone anyone to
Just love me
It was that important to me
I looked for others to give me what
I neglected to provide for me
Someone, anyone, anything

I was begging
to just LOVE me
But first it began in me
Even though I was told God loved me
I couldn't accept that as my reality
Because of all the miseries I seen
So God sent me angels without wings to show me
What it feels like when He loves me
In every word spoke
Every finger stroked
They taught me what to be loved really means
An in every tear shed
Those angels walked back through my journey with me
So that I'd see how and where God loved me
And it's unbelievable and unrealistic to me
Because it's by far more beautiful than anything
I ever imagined love to be
The feelings behind loves embrace
are indescribable to me
So when I learned that all along
God was there and He loved me
Genuinely loved me
And when I quit living for them
and simply lived for HIM
Then I too began to learn to love me
And as I did I noticed an increase
in my existence
Self-worth and self-esteem boosted
with my confidence
So if nobody ever again spoke
those 3 words to me
God did and I knew it
There was hope after all because see
God Loved ME

"Worth"

    We started out on this journey not knowing what to expect or what was to come of it. Not looking for anything at all. We traveled together learning and growing along the way. It was through you that I learned to cry and that crying was ok. It was through you that I was able to shed tears that needed to be set free. It was through you that I learned aspects of me that I never thought I would see. It was because of you that I began to learn me. It was through you that I started to see my own beauty and understand my worth. I spent my entire life being a third-class citizen to the needs, wants, and desires of everyone else. I was their toilet. A mere waste dump for all their excess and I took it all in stride. No self-worth, no self-pride, no joy, no peace, no dignity, very little self-respect... I was always settling because I spent so long being a waste land.

    I thought it was all I was worth. I thought it was all I was created for. I stopped dreaming because my dreams never came true or when they got close to looking like a reality it was shattered to pieces. I never thought my happily ever after was possible. What I was given was all that I'd ever be served up. I thought I'd never amount to anything because that's what was always told to me. I didn't believe I was capable of achieving anything significant because I didn't think I was smart enough since I was always told I was ignorant, dumb, and stupid. I second guessed every decision I made and often allowed others to think or decide for me because I didn't want to make the wrong choice. I believed what was said to me. I went through the motions of what needed to be done according to how I thought it needed or should be done.

    The things that hurt or devastated me I stuffed down, buried, and locked away because it was easier to ignore the pain than it was to try to function through it. From you I learned how to deal with the hurts of the past and to shed tears for who I was and what happened. It's not easy facing yourself when you don't even know who you are or where to begin finding you. You taught me how to find myself through all the buried heart aches of life and the blockage that has kept me from living life. I have merely existed in life all this time and through you I am learning how to put myself first. Upgrading to first class has been a long difficult road. Yet you've hung in there with me. In you I learned that I'm valuable. From you I learned how to let go of my past and embrace my future.

You told me to talk. In my head I'm thinking oh that's not too complicated. I was wrong. See you meant to talk about me. If you ask me a question I can answer it. But, I never really just talked about me so I wasn't sure what to say. I didn't think I had much of a story to tell or anything to say that was worth listening to. But not only did you want me to talk you wanted me to tell you everything. Every aspect of my life .You wanted me to trust you. I prayed, I listened, and I nervously did. You are changing my life. At a time where I had checked out and given up you began to shine a light on the darkest places and pieces of my heart and discuss their existence. You taught me that unless I physically caused many of the devastations of my life to happen IT WASN'T MY FAULT.

It was the fault of the person who had done the injustice. I spent most of my life being blamed and blaming myself for something that I had no control over and never knew until now. I was never to blame. That was hard a pill to swallow. There were moments where I wanted to shut down. Completely stop pressing forward and give up. You wouldn't let me. You pushed me...challenged me... forced me to keep talking, keep sharing, and taught me how to breathe through the difficult moments and keep going. You taught me that I was worthy. I was awesome. And not only that I am worth being loved unconditionally but you demonstrated the words that you spoke.... #IAMWORTHY 😊#

I Write

I write because it saves me
It keeps me sane when I feel as though
life's insanities are consuming me
I write for the little girl in me that was
robbed of her little girl glories
I write of my uncertainties
Things I know are here, but care not to see
I write because it's easier to put pen to paper
than to face the girl in the mirror that stares back at me
I write because often times my words are so much prettier
than the woman I see when I look at me
So I Write......

I allow my men to work as my inspired lyrics
write a sensational melody
I write of my most sacred journeys
Like a Christian at the altar on their knees
I write as swift as the air I breath
I express those inner thoughts
beaten and suppressed in me
You know the memories of you when you
cried night after night of all doubts
When the doctors stuck their tools through
your fetuses head and pulled it out
You know the night you screamed and hollered
Remember what I'm talking about
I write to share the memories of you
When attempted to act on vision of taking my virginity
When you were supposed to be my family
When you profilied about the great things
God had given you to see
When all along all you were after was my body
I write of the miseries I had inside of me
The one that kept enlightening any desire to die

because misery had so much company
I write of my many attempts to commit suicide
Tired of so many times being
abused and casted aside
I write to stitch together my life
To clean my mind, body, and soul
Free my temple of all its stress and strife
I write to give thanks to everyone
God has placed beside me
Without the supporters in my heart
I truly would not be
For the true prophetic visions even I could see
To God I give the glory for in darkness
He was more than just my light

"Write Today"

As much as writing meant to me... as much comfort that it brought me throughout the years, as soothing as it was to me over time and as many tears as it washed away in my pages I quit. I checked out and quit. When I stopped writing it made for some really dark days but I just couldn't bring myself to write again. Then I met someone whom I've grown to absolutely adore and as we sat and talked she told me I needed to write. I still couldn't do it though. But every time I opened my mouth to vent about something or to share a thought, she'd say write it down. I'd shake my head and still wouldn't listen. I thought that part of me was dead and gone. She helped me see that me and my writings hadn't lost each other. All I needed to do was put pen to pad and write again.

When I did I discovered a love for it that ran deeper than anything I've ever known before. She later became one of my greatest inspirations. Every day she helps me move one step closer toward becoming the woman that I desire to be. She is beauty, brains, and success all wrapped up in one package. I want to get on her level one day. I love our conversations because although all of them aren't always easy to have they are beneficial. They make you think. They make you want to be better. They challenge you to strive for more. They make you feel like a warrior that can conquer anything. They make you feel fearless even if sometimes it's just for a moment. They are encouraging, inspiring, motivating, and sometimes downright hilarious. Every so often they are even annoying but I love them all and wouldn't have it any other way. She is persistent.

I don't know what all she sees in me. But, I know that whatever it is, she's going to do everything she can to see every ounce of me operating in my fullest potential... by any means necessary. Every morning for the last maybe three weeks parts of our conversation have been repetitive. I know she doesn't even realize it but it begins in the morning with a wake up text message. She tells me to get up and be productive that day because I have writing to do 😊. Then shortly after that, when I am actually up and moving we are on the phone talking and laughing as usual.

That's until we hit a moment of silence that she'll break by asking "so are you going to write today?" "Ah I didn't plan on it..." "well why not?" "I don't know I just didn't". Then we proceed to talk about something else. Later on in the morning or early afternoon we'll talk again and at random she'll say "did you write today?" I'll respond with "no I didn't write today". Later on that night we talk again and at random she'll say "so did you write today?" "No, I didn't write today. " "Why not?" "I don't know I just didn't". Every day we repeated this until I changed my responses. "Are you going to write today?" "Yes, I'm going to write today". "Good". But she still followed up later in the day with "So did you start writing yet?" If I said "no" she'll ask "why not?" "It got busy". "Oh ok then". Later that night she'll say "so did you write yet?" "I'm writing now". "Awesome."

Eventually I asked her why she always asking me if I was writing. She said because I had a lot to say I needed to get it out. I laughed and didn't give it much thought at first but, I realized that from that moment on every day I was writing. Every day she still checked in to make sure I was writing. I think that was because she knew some of the things I desired to do. She knew what she saw every time she looked at me. So, that was her way of pushing me outside of my head to begin the process and put it on paper. Between us talking and me writing again I began to see a lot of life through a different set of lenses. I loved these conversations and if I ever said "no", it would be a red flag to her that something was wrong.

When I write I'm able to clear my head and put on paper things that I might not ordinarily say out loud. But when I quit talking I quit writing too and I become trapped inside my head. She holds me accountable for everything I do and don't do. No matter what I'm doing she's right there to keep me focused and keep me encouraged. On those really awful days she makes me laugh until tears fall. If for some reason our journey together ever ends I have enough of her in my heart to achieve for both of us. She will forever be a part of me. I love her beyond words. She's like the she in me I desire to be and more. She is the reason I started writing again.

#my Hero#
#my real life warrior princess#
#my cherished blessing#
#a piece of my heart#

God or Nothing

Too many times
I've spent my life in the shadows
Hiding behind the sorrows
of those future stealing souls
And lied empty on the inside
While my secrets coincided with a misery
intertwining within me
And even though my life consists
of more pains than I care to see
I realize for the first time since my mama died
That it's GOD or Nothing
And as long as He's before me
it doesn't matter who's against me
Because behind every storm
there's a silver lining containing a rainbow
So even in the midnight hour
when I begin to grow sick and tired
of being
Sick and Tired
And my tears form pools
of baptisms on my pillow
I'll still refuse to feed
depressions fuel anymore
Therefore, until I reach the end
I must keep pushing
And in pushing
I'll begin to **P**ray **U**ntil **S**omething **H**appens
I'll increase my mustard seed
and blindly leap out on faith
And like Job I too will overcome
some of the brutal heart wrenching obstacles
But I see right now
that most of ya'll don't understand me
I've been mentally, physically,

spiritually, and sexually abused
Torn apart, destroyed, and misused
But how many of ya'll know
that even the broken GOD can use
Yes even the broken down GOD can still use
Cause He did it for me
I was living in bondage, confused,
and in too deep to see reality
I was one of the wolves in sheep's clothing
Sacrificing myself for a glimpse
of a world that seemed like a better life to me
Every day released a bigger part of my soul
Played church trying to find GOD
until He broke me down
And reconstructed my incompletes into a whole
And in doing so
If He never chooses to do another thing
It will forever remain to be GOD or Nothing!

"The Lesson"

In life nothing's fair and nothing comes easy. Nothing's handed to you on a silver platter or wrapped perfectly with a bow. If you really want to accomplish anything you'll have to work hard to achieve it. Along the way you'll come across some cruel, mean, cold hearted people and not just children, but there are many adults out there that are worse than the children. They make elementary school obscenities seem like a bed of roses compared to the negativity that comes from them. If your self - esteem is low and life has taken you on so many winding roads that it's left you totally open and vulnerable, their negativity will engulf you. It will swallow you whole and destroy you as if you never existed. Life don't hold no punches morning, noon, and night. It continuously gives you its all.

So if you're wise, you'll learn early to bob and weave so that life can't knock you out like it almost did me. Everybody goes through something and some worse than others so stop feeling like you're the story yet to be told. There even came a time in my life where the only reason I had sex was because I had been down so many rough roads of physical and mental abuse that I figured if I freely gave it away then no one could ever again take from me something that I didn't want to give. I discovered I was wrong when it happened again. Some people just need more power and control and sometimes there's nothing you can do about it. I felt like I was dying on the inside and fighting for freedom on the outside. I couldn't understand why I wouldn't and couldn't let them devour me but I was fighting for a life I wasn't even 100% sure I actually wanted. But, I did know that there were certain pains I never wanted to feel again and I blamed me for everything that happened in my life. The fact that I thought it was my fault magnified everything I felt on the inside and impacted me in more ways then I knew.

Thinking back... if I didn't get away from certain church folk when I did they would have killed me. See, I didn't know it then but I do now that just because people go to church don't mean that they are all saved. For some, the church folks are the closet things they've got to Jesus and they're writing themselves a one way ticket to hell so you've got to know God for yourself. Develop your own relationship with Him and not base your walk with Christ off the walk of someone else. I learned everything in church except Jesus. See, church held my firsts of everything and everything I learned in church I took out to the world to get paid for it. In the process though, they also destroyed what little I did have on the inside of me. I didn't have much confidence because I was never taught how to. I didn't sit down with anyone who talked to me about self- worth, self-pride and self-dignity. But, I was a chameleon so I learned as I went by imitating the people around me that said they loved me.

    The world was my stage and I was the world's greatest actress on it because I could appear to be great but behind closed doors my life told a totally different story. My life was being written one moment at a time and the pages told a totally different story than the images you saw in real life. Too often we as a people make the mistake of feeling like just because we got out of a situation we got over it. But, that's not always the case. Just because you go through hurt, pain, sorrow, or a devastating experience, in the midst of the storms you have to fight. You have to fight in the physical but you also have fights going on that the people round you can't even see. Many times we have to fight with our depression, our self-esteem, fear, doubt, insecurity and to survive. You have to fight childhood issues that linger into your adult life. All the while you're fighting all these things, you've got people around you that are literally trying to destroy you.

    Dealing with all this and still trying to live... trying to function took its toll on me. I began to see everyone that affected me in my past in everyone that was trying to be a part of my future and I got stuck. I felt like my past was haunting me. I was losing control and couldn't sleep because every time I closed my eyes I saw something that happened. The people that sexually assaulted me... that raped me... were once again grabbing me by my ankles and dragging me out of my bed. It was a dream but in that moment it was real. Everywhere I went... people, touches, scents were all triggers for me that I couldn't cope with. They sent me into flashbacks but in my mind in front of me I saw those same moments all over again. I had to get help because I was once again spiraling out of control real fast.

Death was running on my heels. I almost gave up. I checked out on life but my heart wouldn't let me die. I had to continuously remind myself that I survived. I made it out. I wasn't with those same people anymore. I could no longer figure things out on my own. I needed help. I was worried about me and at the same time someone around me saw me spiraling and sent some help my way. I started seeing a therapist. I didn't understand the importance of talking until I became so trapped inside my own head and unable to find the escape route. I was always the type of person where I held everything in. I disconnected myself from the situation in order to cope. I never addressed the issues. I just pretended like I wasn't hurt and like it didn't bother me or like everything was ok even when it wasn't.

My therapist explained that your mind is like a file cabinet when it comes to painful things. There's only so much you can put in and file. But, eventually the cabinet acts like a 'jack-n-the-box' and wants to get out. You have to start dealing with it then because there's no going back. If you try to put it back in once it has popped out on its own you'll likely end up with more problems than you had originally. This was my issue. I never dealt with anything. I thought that when I got away from a situation I was over it. It wasn't until I couldn't control the triggers and I started getting help that I realized just how many scars and unhealed wounds I had actually developed.

One day, in the middle of an episode I pressed my back against the wall because I needed to feel safe. I needed to feel support. I needed to remind myself that no one was about to get me from behind. In front of me I heard this voice saying to me "It's ok, you're safe, you're in a safe place, tell me where you are, tell me what's happening, what do you see?" I couldn't speak. Tears poured down my face. I was stuck. Scared. Every time I tried to move I couldn't. I'd press my fingertips against the wall one at a time... counting. For a moment I forgot where I was and thought that maybe I ended up back in the same place I escaped from. I didn't know I was there the first time until I was already in it. I cried and prayed "God please don't let me go backwards. There are people around me and in so many of them I see the people I escaped from. I'm trying to do this whole church thing but it's hard. The hugs and touches are driving me crazy. God please don't let me go crazy in front of these people and if any of them mean me harm please keep them away from me." The voice (my therapist) kept talking to me "look at me. It's ok. You're safe. You're in a safe place. I'm going to touch you right now. It's ok. Keep looking at me." I still jumped at the touch. I don't know why I thought I was about to be hit but I did.

These episodes started happening more and more often and I was trying to hide it and pretend like everything was ok. I needed to feel like I was normal but I didn't know how I was gonna make it through most days. But I kept talking. I had to push past what I was feeling and seeing and explain what was happening in those moments. I had to be completely transparent in order to get through it and truly heal from it. I also learned that you can't blame yourself for a situation that is beyond your control unless you can prove how YOU directly caused the action to occur. I try to see my therapist as often as possible because it helps me learn me so that I can become the woman I desire to be. In my life I've experienced more hurt than I have happiness. But no matter what you go through in life always remember this... no matter what the situation looks like... no matter what it feels like... you can overcome it.

Note from The Author:

I've spent a lifetime running backwards trying to leave the past behind only for it to catch up with me. This is because I ignored what I was going through instead of learning how to heal from it. Now I'm learning how to heal. Just like my journey has taken me down various roads, each of these roads created pages in my journal. Pages that though they aren't always easy to digest, I decided to share pieces of my story with you. I'm doing this in hopes that it teaches someone that no matter what hand you're dealt in life or no matter what path you stumble down, in the end life is what you make of it. Don't let your circumstances dictate the final outcome of your journey. As I grow and as I progress I am writing my way through my healing. Some of my pages may be half written and incomplete because that is where I am in my process. Each day I am growing and tackling issues I got away from but never healed from. I am doing the work needed to heal by talking to a therapist.

I'm releasing, crying, and fighting my way to my freedom. Yes, my roads have been rocky and rough. Some paths I almost didn't make it off of. But since I was kept by grace and shown so much mercy, God helped me find my way back. I am far from perfect. I am a continuous work in progress and every day I write. Though therapy is something I never in a million years thought I'd ever be doing, it's been my greatest challenge and biggest reward. It has helped me tremendously in finding out who I really am, understanding me better, and blaming me for situations that were beyond my control a lot less. It has taught me to accept me and love me beyond the broken pieces. It's teaching me how to move myself from a third class to a first-class citizen in my life. It is daring me to move beyond my once stuck places. I'm understanding that who I became is not who I am. It's merely what I created to cope with where I was in order to complete those incomplete pages and heal the hidden wounds and scars that were buried when I escaped instead of confronting what I couldn't deal with. I look forward to seeing what new paths await as I am entering into a new chapter in my life. I am longing for my restoration process while on this course of putting the broken pieces back together again.

About the Author

Arketa Williams is the Founder of Pen2Pad Ink Publishing and Co-Founder of Infinity Empowerment & Development Corp. (IEDC), a community development and outreach organization.

She is also an author, poet, transformational coach, and inspiration to many. She has been writing for over 22 years. Her writing is more than simply telling a story or writing a beautifully crafted poem. It's the essence of who she is. Her pen was her voice when she didn't have one. Now she vividly paints pictures of struggle and triumph with words as a way of showing people that no matter how difficult the journey, you can overcome anything. She has received numerous awards and recognitions throughout the years for her creativity. She has also been published in several anthologies.

Arketa has an Associate's degree in Business and a Bachelor's degree in Business Administration and General Management. While working on her degrees she published her first two books entitled No More Midnight Tears and Shhhh.... I Know. She later went on to publish A Hidden Heart and Fists of Rage. In May of 2017 she released part 1 of a duo entitled A Sinner's Circle. She has also released a CD of poetry entitled

Behind the Shadows of Your Heart and a DVD entitled It Is Spoken.

She is currently working on her next series of books of poetry and novels. Arketa has turned her poetry into a lyrical lifestyle of mental freedom and uses her escape from trials and tribulations as a ray of hope for those stranded where she used to be. She does this in order to let the world know that there is sunshine after the storm. She has blessed the lives of people throughout various cities and states and continues to be an inspiration to people everywhere.

For bookings or to contact her please email contact@pen2padink.org. She can also be found on Facebook, Instagram, and Twitter at Author Arketa Williams.

www.ingramcontent.com/pod-product-compliance
Lightning Source LLC
Chambersburg PA
CBHW030331080526
44584CB00012B/817